Marcus Tullius Cicero, Alfred Pretor

Letters of Cicero to Atticus

Vol. 1

Marcus Tullius Cicero, Alfred Pretor

Letters of Cicero to Atticus
Vol. 1

ISBN/EAN: 9783744718233

Printed in Europe, USA, Canada, Australia, Japan

Cover: Foto ©Thomas Meinert / pixelio.de

More available books at **www.hansebooks.com**

THE
LETTERS OF CICERO TO ATTICUS.

BOOK I.

WITH NOTES AND AN ESSAY ON THE CHARACTER OF THE AUTHOR.

EDITED BY

ALFRED PRETOR, M.A.,
(LATE OF TRINITY COLLEGE),
FELLOW OF ST CATHARINE'S COLLEGE, CAMBRIDGE.

NEW EDITION REVISED.

Cambridge:
DEIGHTON, BELL, AND CO.
LONDON: G. BELL AND SONS.
1882.

PREFACE.

THE following text has been formed by a careful comparison of the editions of Schütz, Ernesti, Klotz, Nobbe and Boot. In some of the more important letters I am indebted likewise to Matthiae and the more recent edition of Mr Watson. In respect to the notes, if in any case I have borrowed without an acknowledgment, I have done so only when it was impossible to verify the actual author from the many who had adopted his results at second-hand. For the arrangement of the letters I should much have preferred the chronological order of Schütz, but, though indispensable if the edition had been a complete one, it would have been of little real advantage in editing a fragment like the present.

My best thanks are due to Mr W. W. Radcliffe, Fellow of King's College, for his kindness in undertaking to revise the sheets for the Press.

One word in conclusion on the vexed question of translations. If a schoolboy is sufficiently advanced to be reading Cicero's Letters, he is past the stage at which his scholarship will be injured by a bad translation, while his style may gain much from a good one. Accordingly for the amount of translation contained in the notes I offer no apology: for its shortcomings as a translation, many.

It is also my hope that the more continuous passages may be found available for teaching Latin Prose by the only sure method, that of retranslation.

ST CATHARINE'S COLLEGE,
January, 1873.

ON THE CHARACTER OF CICERO.

A biography of Cicero is no desideratum, when such authorities on the subject as Mommsen, Merivale and Forsyth are accessible to every schoolboy: but on the question of his character, there seems as little prospect as ever of a unanimous verdict, and, while this is so, an editor can scarcely do otherwise than range himself with one or other of the two contending parties. My own opinion, formed at school under circumstances and teaching the least likely to foster it, that Cicero's character is a weak and a selfish one, has only been confirmed by a more careful study of his works: nor can I read the panegyrics which have been lavished upon him without a real feeling of surprise that such scanty materials should have been found sufficient for the construction of this gigantic idol. In their judgment of this one man, his critics have tacitly ignored the ordinary canons by which men measure goodness, justice and the like, and, in their desire to do him honour, have invented an arbitrary interpretation for the most negative and commonplace characteristics. Words and actions the most trivial and the most unfrequent are thrown out in strong relief, and quoted triumphantly in support of his character:

while glimpses of affection for a son, a daughter, or a friend,—sufficiently rare if we consider the circumstances, and, if they were twice as numerous, still not peculiar to Cicero,—are appealed to as evincing extraordinary goodness of heart. In a word, on the strength of a few isolated passages we are required to silence what I venture to say is, in nine cases out of ten, the primary conviction of the reader, that these are the records of a man who in his private relations was vain, selfish and unaffectionate, and in his public life a weak and unprincipled time-server.

Neither can I give in my adherence to a dictum often quoted by his admirers, that so large a correspondence as that left by Cicero is a hard test by which to regulate our judgment of a man's life and character. The question is at all events a debateable one, even as regards his public life, for many an act of political scheming might gain rather than lose by an insight into the motives which actuated it. That Cicero's politics rarely *do* gain by the light thus thrown upon them, is, I take it, strong testimony that the motives which inspired them were unworthy rather than the reverse, ambitious and self-interested rather than pure and patriotic. On the other hand I am certain that to a man of ordinary goodness and kindness of heart, the loss, if any, to his political reputation by the publication of his private correspondence would be more than counterbalanced by the pleasant kindly traits of character which could hardly fail to betray themselves in his moments of unreserve. This test I shall presently apply to our author, with what results I leave the reader to determine.

Of actual immorality, nothing, in so far as I know, can be proved against Cicero, a fact which I should be tempted to ascribe in some measure to the want of force in his character, whether for good or evil. More probably it arose from a regard for his own dignity, and, if so, it is the most praiseworthy product of that self-love which meets us at every turn in his character.

It cannot at any rate have been due to principle or conscientiousness on his part, when we see the easy terms on which he could temporize with vice in others, and how eagerly he coveted the friendship of men the most profligate and the most unscrupulous[1], thereby affording an indirect encouragement to vice for which even his warmest admirers must hold him responsible. To account for the contrary view, which till quite recently has held its ground, I can only suggest the force of tradition, and the sympathy which is so naturally excited in his favour by the malice of his enemies and his untimely death.

But it is time to proceed to more direct charges, amongst which let me notice in the first place the count of *political immorality;* by which I am far from implying that we shall detect him in any flagrant act of criminality, such as now and again proves a fatal blemish to an otherwise fair reputation. For instance, though lavish in his expenditure to a fault, he was not avaricious, and in the case of his provincial administration his conduct appears to have been in marked contrast with the extortionate proceedings of most of

His political immorality

---

[1] In addition to the more flagrant case of Antonius this is also true of his relations with Crassus (*ad Att.* I. 14. 4), Clodius (*ad Att.* II. 1. 5), and others of the same class (*ad Att.* I. 19. 8).

the Roman officials. But, granting this, he had yet nothing of the high principle which was so conspicuous in Cato and Catulus, to keep him straight amidst a mass of conflicting interests, and, as a consequence, he was perpetually betrayed into a time-serving policy utterly unworthy of himself and most prejudicial to his influence for good. Nothing illustrates this fact more clearly than his conduct throughout the Clodian prosecution. Having set the matter in motion he is alarmed the next moment at the probable consequences, and would gladly have compromised it, had compromise been possible. Failing which, he drops quietly out of the case, and leaves the real work of the prosecution to be undertaken by Cato, Cornificius and others, himself the while looking on. It is useless for Abeken to plead in his defence that 'he could not take in a case at once,' when we have his own express statement that his conduct was the result of premeditation[1]. More than this he appreciated, no one better, the real crises of the prosecution, to the first of which he alludes in a passage of the fourteenth letter[2], while on the second and far more important occasion, when Hortensius proposed his scheme for the reconstitution of the court[3], Cicero kept a resolute silence, though taking credit to himself for having foreseen

as shewn by his conduct in the prosecution of Clodius,

---

[1] Cf. *ad Att.* I. 13. 3 *nosmet ipsi, qui Lycurgei a principio fuissemus, quotidie demitigamur.*

[2] *ad Att.* I. 14. 5 *tabellae ministrabantur ita ut nulla daretur* UTI ROGAS. *Hic tibi rostra Cato advolat, convicium Pisoni consuli mirificum facit: si id est convicium, vox plena gravitatis, plena auctoritatis, plena denique salutis.*

[3] *ad Att.* I. 16. 2 *posteaquam vero Hortensius excogitavit ut legem de religione Fufius tribunus plebis ferret......contraxi vela perspiciens inopiam iudicum, neque dixi quidquam pro testimonio, nisi quod erat ita notum atque testatum ut non possem praeterire.*

from the first its fatal tendency. It is scarcely too much to say that a bold speech at this moment in defence of the original measure would have altered his own future, and perhaps even the future of Rome. But instead of this he temporized with every party in turn, till the case had slipped out of his hands: immediately after which he launched out into idle invective, every word of which made him an enemy for life, while it was utterly ineffective in recovering the confidence of his friends.

In this case at any rate it was not from a want of prescience that he erred—for he foresaw the issue: nor yet from a want of courage—for he was courageous enough when courage was useless: but simply and solely from a want of principle. Having no high standard of right to which to refer his actions he cringed to each party in succession, till he had so tied his hands with conflicting obligations that he could only sit down in silence and see the maze unravel itself by agencies over which he had lost the control. And the story repeats itself in the case of the knights of Asia and the bribery commissions[1], on both of which occasions the conduct of Cato is in splendid contrast with his own, and again in the trials of Macer[2], Catilina[3] and Antonius[4], all of which are so many additional proofs that interest and not principle formed the standard of his actions.

in the case of the bribery commissions, of the Asiani equites and the trials of Catilina, Macer and Antonius.

---

[1] *ad Att.* II. 1. 8 *quid verius quam in iudicium venire, qui ob rem iudicandam pecuniam acceperit? censuit hoc Cato: assensit senatus. equites curiae bellum, non mihi: nam ego dissensi. quid impudentius publicanis renuntiantibus? fuit tamen, retinendi ordinis causa, facienda iactura. restitit et pervicit Cato.*
[2] *ad Att.* I. 4. 2.   [3] *ad Att.* I. 2. 1.
[4] *ad Att.* I. 12. 2.

Neither can it be said that he was averse to bribes, when offered in the shape of office[1], for of money and houses he had enough and to spare. His shortcomings on this head have, I know, been excused on the ground of precedent and the usage of the times: another plea with which I have but little sympathy, for the times were not so destitute of good examples as it is the fashion to suppose: while, if he is to justify the praise of his admirers, he must be proved to have led, rather than to have followed, the multitude.

May I take it for granted that the above examples have at any rate proved this fact, that Cicero was unscrupulous in the use of his means? The question follows, what was the ultimate aim and object for which he was content to sacrifice honour and self-respect? His *immediate* object in dropping the Clodian prosecution was unquestionably and by his own admission[2] to prevent at any cost the disunion of the optimates and the collapse of the existing government. We have therefore only to determine whether his *ulterior* motive was a patriotic or a self-interested one.

Self-interest the ruling principle of his life.

Taking as I do the worse view of his character, my object will be to prove, if possible, that he foresaw throughout the doom of the existing administration and appreciated its worthlessness and corruption, yet continued notwithstanding to give it his most unqualified support for two reasons, (i) because he considered it the best field for the display of his powers, and (ii) because he wanted time to forecast the future and to shape his own conduct accordingly. This view of his character, which is as old as the time of Dio

---

[1] *ad Att.* II. 18. 3, and again II. 5. 2.
[2] *ad Att.* II. 1. 8.

Cassius[1], is in part adopted by Mr Merivale in the preface to his Life of Cicero, from which I may be pardoned for quoting the following passage: 'It is humiliating to the pretensions of human genius, but it not the less becomes us to acknowledge it, that after all his efforts to purge his mental vision of the films of prejudice, Cicero was blind to the real fact, that his devotion to the commonwealth was grounded not so much upon his conviction of its actual merits, as of its fitness for the display of his own abilities.'

Of the correctness of the above view the following I think are proofs:

(i) His *self-congratulation*[2] at the increase of his own popularity from the failure of the Clodian prosecution, a miscarriage of justice which in the next letter but one he recognises as the death-blow of the commonwealth[3]. *as shewn by his own statement,*

(ii) His *conduct in exile*, which is to me inexplicable except on the one supposition that he had been throughout his life working for himself and not for his country, and, as in the days of his prosperity he had thought and spoken of the republic only in reference to himself and his consulship, so when his reverses came upon him his concern for its dissolution was swallowed up in a purely selfish sorrow for himself and his losses. *by his conduct in exile.*

(iii) His *friendship with Pompeius*, in connection with which we shall do well to remember the following facts:—that it was *and by his relations with Pompeius.*

---

[1] Dio Cass. XXXVI. 25, a passage of which Mr Merivale gives the following translation: '[Cicero] was a mere timeserver and passed now to one side now to the other in order to curry favour alternately with each.' There is nothing more extraordinary than the deliberate way in which the verdict of antiquity on Cicero's character has been habitually ignored.

[2] *ad Att.* I. 16. 11.

[3] *ad Att.* I. 16. 6, and again I. 18. 3.

closely preceded by the bitterest enmity towards him: that it had its origin in a period when even the least practised eye must have seen that no one man could any longer save the republic, and that Cicero acknowledges the fact in the very letters in which he congratulates himself on having secured Pompeius as his patron: that he was clearly heartbroken at the downfall of this friend[1], yet was at the same time able to use the most temperate language over the ruin of the commonwealth[2], nay even to congratulate himself that the claims of Pompeius with posterity would no longer outweigh his own[3]. In a word, I cannot believe that he was induced to court Pompeius in preference to Caesar, or Cato, or Clodius, by any motive except self-interest and a mistaken idea that he was the man of the future, for he knew his character[4] and his aims[5], while of faith in his political professions, under cover of which the alliance between them was formed, Cicero by his own admission had little or none. Even Abeken admits that the conduct of Pompeius 'ought to have opened the eyes of every unprejudiced person,' while, as regards his own motives, Cicero is sufficiently explicit in the following passages: *'sed tamen, quoniam ista sunt infirma, munitur quaedam nobis ad retinendas opes nostras tuta, ut spero, via, quam tibi litteris satis explicare non possum; significatione parva ostendam tamen. utor Pompeio familiarissime* (I. 17. 10), and again: *putavi mihi maiores quasdam opes*

---

[1] *ad Att.* II. 21. 3.
[2] *ad Att.* II. 21. 2, and II. 9 I *festive, mihi crede, et minore sonitu quam putaram orbis hic in republica est conversus.*
[3] *ad Att.* II. 17, 2.
[4] *ad Att.* I. 13. 4, and again I. 20. 2.
[5] *ad Att.* II. 17. 1.

et firmiora praesidia esse quaerenda (I. 19. 7), and again: *si vero quae de me pacta sunt ea non servantur, in caelo sum, ut sciat hic noster Hierosolymarius traductor ad plebem quam bonam meis putissimis orationibus gratiam retulerit* (II. 9. 1).

Supposing the above to be a true explanation of his conduct, then the one fatal mistake of his life was made when he swore allegiance to Pompeius instead of to Caesar: a mistake which must have cost him many pangs as he dallied in turn with the offer of of a legation (II. 18. 3) and an augurship (II. 5. 2)[1], with the dread before his eyes of what posterity six hundred years later would say if he adventured this last and most shameless transfer of his allegiance (II. 5. 1).

On his incapacity as a statesman there is little need to dwell at length, for the fact is generally admitted, and some of its more prominent features have already been incidentally illustrated, e. g. his want of prevision in the selection of Pompeius as the man of the future, and his want of tact in the useless exasperation of a triumphant foe. Of his inconsistency in politics the present book supplies us with two striking examples: the first in the case of the Clodian trial, when to the announcement of his own irresolution he appends the remarkable words, 'In a word, I am afraid that this outrage neglected by the well disposed and upheld by the vicious will prove a fertile source of disasters to the state:' the next when he comments with great bitterness on the collapse of a bribery bill[2], totally ignoring the fact that it was owing to

His incapacity as a statesman shewn by his want of foresight, his want of tact,

his inconsistency.

---

[1] *quo quidem uno ab istis capi possum.*
[2] *ad Att.* I. 18. 3 *facto senatus consulto de ambitu, de iudiciis: nulla lex perlata.*

his own determined opposition that the measure in question had never become law.

and his indecision. But it is to his indecision, which was with him the rule rather than the exception, that his failure as a politician is mainly to be attributed. In the suppression of the Catilinarian conspiracy, to which his friends so triumphantly appeal, it will be necessary to bear in mind two facts, (1) that it happened at an early stage of his political career when his interests were less conflicting, and his path consequently more clear: (2) that we have after all little else than his own account of the transaction, for the speeches of Crassus and Pompeius and his other admirers in the senate are so clearly self-interested as to be almost grotesque in their extravagance and utterly worthless as evidence. But, in whatever light we may regard his services on this particular occasion, the fact remains the same, that his politics as a rule were characterised by habitual indecision—the result, it may be, of natural weakness of character bewildered by the conflicting interests of a selfish ambition —and it was this more than anything else which alienated his friends and in the end left him in almost total isolation. Whatever his ultimate object may have been, it is at any rate certain that he had never formed a definite plan for its attainment, and having no policy he had soon as a consequence no party. The men of action on the other hand, as for instance Caesar and Pompeius, were daily adding to the number of their followers. Even Cato the most uncompromising, and Clodius the most unprincipled, of men were not without their partisans. Cicero alone had no adherents on whom he could rely, though at the outset of his political career numbers were unquestionably predisposed in his favour by the popularity of his cause. But this promise was soon belied, and they left him to strengthen other factions when all clue to his conduct was lost in a maze of inconsistency and vacillation. Reactions it is true at times took place in his favour, (*concursus* or *rallyings* is his own expression), according as he gave glimpses of a more manly and straightforward policy, but, often as these were repeated, I cannot accept them as evidence that he had secured any lasting hold on the affections even of a few. In every single instance we can trace, I think, the signs of a momentary admiration, oftener still of interested motives, but never a symptom of that steady unwavering confidence by which alone a man of Cicero's temperament could have been nerved for any sustained effort.

A friendly critic[1] has summed up the character of Cicero in these words: 'Nor can we wonder, however much we may lament it, that in times so corrupt as these even Cicero should not have been altogether free from prevalent errors and defects. His early connection with Catilina has been already noticed, and the compact not less discreditable which existed apparently between him and Antonius, as likewise his defence of that worthless man who had committed such illegal acts in Macedonia. We are surprised also at the lukewarmness he at first[2] (!) manifested in the case of Clodius: nor finally can we fail to be struck with the conscious pride and satisfaction, deserving no better name

His vanity and selfishness in his private relations with Atticus and others.

---

[1] Abeken.
[2] The note of admiration is my own. I have already quoted the words of Cicero: 'nosmet ipsi, qui Lycurgei *a principio* fuissemus, quotidie demitigamur.'

than vanity, which obtrudes itself upon us in many passages of his letters.'

With the criticism so far I am of course altogether agreed, for the bitterest enemy of Cicero could not have summed up his political offences in a more brief and telling catalogue. But to the defence which the writer proceeds to set up, if defence it can be called, I take the strongest possible exception. 'On the other hand (he says) our reprobation of these failings is in a great measure softened by the candour and freedom with which he discusses all his concerns with his friend.'

Even if the assumption be true on which our allowance is claimed, the claim at any rate is inadmissible in Cicero's case, whose egotism is not of a character to be excused on these grounds. When I see how entirely his correspondence with Atticus is leavened with vanity, far from finding any excuse in the fact, I can only argue how deeply the vice must have been engrained in his nature when it finds expression in his letters to a most intimate friend, the very last place in the world where one would expect it to appear. For in the intercourse with a friend, who knows your every thought, self-assertion should naturally find no place, and it is inveterate vanity indeed that will still declare itself when the motive for so doing has ceased to exist. On the other hand, if a man has any unselfishness in his disposition it will nowhere more certainly appear than in a familiar correspondence of this kind. Unfortunately the passages in which Cicero shows a really disinterested affection as distinct from the merely formal compliments in use between acquaintances are wonderfully few and far between. Else why quote isolated examples, as his admirers do, of a feeling which, to be worth anything, ought to constitute the tone of the entire correspondence? For instance, the editors are loud in their praise of his affection for his brother and his daughter, and of the sorrow he displays at the death of an intimate companion. But surely there is nothing specially characteristic of Cicero in these feelings, which we may fairly assume to have been not altogether unknown to men like Catilina and Clodius.

On the other hand there are at least three passages[1] in this book alone, in which such a feeling is only conspicuous by its absence; and, even when these have been explained away, the whole tone of the letters is selfish still. Nine tenths of the book are occupied with himself and his own concerns. With the exception of Atticus, no one, save the two or three persons to whom I have already alluded, is mentioned with any degree of interest, and in the management of the one important concern with which he had been entrusted by Atticus he is dilatory and neglectful, and at last dismisses it from his mind with an unsympathising comment[2]. And as regards affection for his friend, I can see little signs of it beyond the usual stereotyped commonplaces: and that Atticus felt the omission is plain from the very remarkable passage at the commencement of *Ep.* XVII., which, so far from being an honest exhibition of feeling, is no better than a vote of confidence delivered at the pressing request of his friend. (Cf. § 7 of the letter in

---

[1] *Ep.* VI. 2 if we accept the reading *decessit*, *Ep.* XI. 1, and *Ep.* XVII. 7.
[2] *sed haec aut sanabuntur quum veneris, aut ei molesta erunt in utro culpa erit.*

question.) But the most significant fact of all is that throughout these sixteen books of letters we are kept in almost total ignorance of Atticus and his concerns. I should scarcely have thought it possible to write four letters, much less four hundred, to a friend in whom one was deeply interested, without introducing questions and allusions which would have enabled the reader in some degree to picture to himself his occupation and habits. On the part of Atticus at any rate there was no such want of sympathy, as may be gathered from the pointed questions in reference to his friend's doings, which are noticed and answered by Cicero in almost every letter. But on the other side there is certainly no response of sympathy. The allusions of Cicero to his friend's occupations are of the most meagre and unsatisfactory kind, shuffled as a rule into three or four lines at the end of a letter, and withal so devoid of interest that to the end of the chapter Atticus is little else to the reader than an epistolary dummy, on which are hung the trophies of Cicero's life. If this view of his character be the correct one, we are at no loss to account for his own statement, that, with the exception of Atticus, he had no real friend. And in this lay one of the great secrets of his weakness, for it is most certain that no man ever needed them more. Cicero was not one who could mark out his path and pursue it independently of counsel and advice. Even in these letters we see at every turn the childlike reliance he places on the discretion and foresight of Atticus, and can gather that his was beyond question a character which the devotion of a few true friends might have strengthened to do great things, and which, for lack of them, was in its political aspect

Failure, crowning failure, failure from end to end.

One word in conclusion on the aim of the foregoing pages. To have attempted to prove my point by an examination in detail of Cicero's life and writings would have been clearly beyond the scope of the present edition, which deals with a fragment only of his works. It would also have been foreign to my purpose, which was not so much to supplement and rearrange the existing materials, as to modify if possible the conclusions which are usually drawn from them, as they are already supplied to us by the author himself and by any one of his numerous biographers. Cases in which he sacrificed truth and honesty to the interests of a party, or of an individual, could be multiplied out of the letters *ad infinitum*, but to what end? The few I have selected as typical from the present book will prove as conclusively as a thousand that in his eyes morality was secondary to expedience: and, if the plan of this edition has prevented me from noticing some points which might have told in his favour, it has at least prevented me from dwelling on that portion of his life, which is of all others the one most difficult to be excused or palliated, I mean his relations with Caesar, and his unseemly exultation at his death. In this, as in the other crises of his life, the difficulties of his position may be allowed to extenuate his failings, but not to exalt his failings into virtues: and what I most earnestly desire to combat is the special pleading of Abeken and others, which, while it admits that he was a vain and immoral statesman, can yet attempt to excuse all this on the shallowest of pleas and to elevate him anew to the position of a hero and a patriot. For myself, with the exception of his marvellous powers as an orator and writer, I can, I confess, see little in our author to command our admiration or respect.

I.

(Romae. Cotta, Torquato coss. 689.)

Cicero Attico S.

1. Petitionis nostrae, quam tibi summae curae esse scio, huius modi ratio est, quod adhuc coniectura provideri possit. prensat unus P. Galba. sine fuco ac fallaciis, more maiorum, negatur. ut opinio est hominum, non aliena rationi nostrae fuit illius haec praepropera prensatio. nam illi ita negant vulgo, ut mihi se debere dicant. ita quiddam spero nobis profici, quum hoc percrebrescit, plurimos nostros amicos inveniri. nos autem initium prensandi facere cogitaramus eo ipso tempore, quo tuum puerum cum his litteris proficisci Cincius dicebat, in campo, comitiis tribuniciis, a. d. XVI Kalend. Sext. competitores, qui certi esse videantur, Galba et Antonius et Q. Cornificius. puto te in hoc aut risisse aut ingemuisse. ut frontem ferias, sunt qui etiam Caesonium putent. Aquilium non arbitramur, qui denegat et iuravit morbum et illud suum regnum iudiciale opposuit. Catilina, si iudicatum erit meridie non lucere, certus erit competitor. de Auli filio et Palicano non puto te exspectare dum scribam. 2. de iis, qui nunc petunt, Caesar certus putatur. Thermus cum Silano contendere existimatur: qui sic inopes et ab amicis et existimatione sunt, ut mihi videatur non esse ἀδύνατον Curium obducere. sed hoc praeter me

nemini videtur. nostris rationibus maxime conducere videtur Thermum fieri cum Caesare. nemo est enim ex iis, qui nunc petunt, qui si in nostrum annum reciderit firmior candidatus fore videatur, propterea quod curator est viae Flaminiae, quae tunc erit absoluta. †sane facile et libenter eum cum Caesare consulem factum viderim. petitorum haec est adhuc informata cogitatio. nos in omni munere candidatorio fungendo summam adhibebimus diligentiam et fortasse, quoniam videtur in suffragiis multum posse Gallia, quum Romae a iudiciis forum refrixerit, excurremus mense Septembri legati ad Pisonem, ut Ianuario revertamur. quum perspexero voluntates nobilium, scribam ad te. caetera spero prolixa esse, his dumtaxat urbanis competitoribus. illam manum tu mihi cura ut praestes, quoniam propius abes, Pompeii, nostri amici. nega me ei iratum fore, si ad mea comitia non venerit. atque haec huius modi sunt. 3. sed est quod abs te mihi ignosci pervelim. Caecilius, avunculus tuus, a P. Vario quum magna pecunia fraudaretur, agere coepit cum eius fratre A. Caninio Satrio de iis rebus, quas eum dolo malo mancipio accepisse de Vario diceret. una agebant caeteri creditores, in quibus erat Lucullus et P. Scipio et is, quem putabant magistrum fore, si bona venirent, L. Pontius. verum hoc ridiculum est de magistro nunc cognoscere. rogavit me Caecilius, ut adessem contra Satrium. dies fere nullus est quin hic Satrius domum meam ventitet. observat L. Domitium maxime: me habet proximum. fuit et mihi et Q. fratri magno usui in nostris petitionibus. 4. sane sum perturbatus quum ipsius Satrii familiaritate tum Domitii, in quo uno maxime ambitio nostra nititur. demonstravi haec Caecilio: simul et illud ostendi, si ipse unus cum illo uno contenderet, me ei satis facturum fuisse: nunc in causa universorum creditorum, hominum praesertim amplissimorum, qui sine eo, quem Caecilius suo nomine perhiberet, facile communem causam sustinerent, aequum esse eum et officio meo consulere et tempori. durius accipere hoc mihi visus est quam vellem et quam homines belli solent et postea prorsus ab instituta nostra paucorum dierum consuetudine longe refugit. abs te peto, ut mihi hoc ignoscas et me existimes humanitate esse prohibitum, ne contra amici summam existimationem miserrimo eius tempore venirem, quum is omnia sua studia et officia in me contulisset. quod si voles in me esse durior, ambitionem mihi putabis obstitisse. ego autem arbitror, etiam si id sit, mihi ignoscendum esse: ἐπεὶ οὐχ ἱερήϊον οὐδὲ βοείην. vides enim in quo cursu simus et quam omnes gratias non modo retinendas verum etiam acquirendas putemus. spero tibi me causam probasse: cupio quidem certe. 5. Hermathena tua valde me delectat et posita ita belle est ut totum gymnasium eius ἀνάθημα esse videatur. multum te amamus.

II.

(Romae. Cotta, Torquato coss. 689.)

CICERO ATTICO S.

1. L. Iulio Caesare C. Marcio Figulo consulibus filiolo me auctum scito salva Terentia. abs te tam,

diu nihil litterarum? ego de meis ad te rationibus scripsi antea diligenter. hoc tempore Catilinam, competitorem nostrum, defendere cogitamus. iudices habemus, quos volumus, summa accusatoris voluntate. spero, si absolutus erit, coniunctiorem illum nobis fore in ratione petitionis: sin aliter acciderit, humaniter feremus. 2. tuo adventu nobis opus est maturo: nam prorsus summa hominum est opinio tuos familiares, nobiles homines, adversarios nostro honori fore. ad eorum voluntatem mihi conciliandam maximo te mihi usui fore video. qua re Ianuario ineunte, ut constituisti, cura ut Romae sis.

III.

(Romae. Cotta, Torquato coss. 689.)

CICERO ATTICO S.

1. Aviam tuam scito desiderio tui mortuam esse et simul quod verita sit ne Latinae in officio non manerent et in montem Albanum hostias non adducerent. eius rei consolationem ad te L. Saufeium missurum esse arbitror. 2. nos hic te ad mensem Ianuarium exspectamus: ex quodam rumore an ex litteris tuis ad alios missis? nam ad me de eo nihil scripsisti. signa, quae nobis curasti, ea sunt ad Caietam exposita. nos ea non vidimus: neque enim exeundi Roma potestas nobis fuit. misimus qui pro vectura solveret. te multum amamus, quod ea abs te diligenter parvoque curata sunt. 3. quod ad me saepe scripsisti de nostro amico placando, feci et expertus sum omnia, sed mirandum in modum est animo abalienato: quibus de suspicionibus,

etsi audisse te arbitror, tamen ex me quum veneris cognosces. Sallustium praesentem restituere in eius veterem gratiam non potui. hoc ad te scripsi, quod is me accusare de te solebat. in se expertus est illum esse minus exorabilem, meum studium nec tibi defuisse. Tulliolam C. Pisoni L. F. Frugi despondimus.

IV.

(Romae. Lepido, Tullo coss. 688.)

CICERO ATTICO S.

1. Crebras exspectationes nobis tui commoves. nuper quidem, quum iam te adventare arbitraremur, repente abs te in mensem Quintilem reiecti sumus. nunc vero censeo, quod commodo tuo facere poteris, venias ad id tempus quod scribis. obieris Quinti fratris comitia, nos longo intervallo viseris, Acutilianam controversiam transegeris. hoc me etiam Peducaeus ut ad te scriberem admonuit: putamus enim utile esse te aliquando iam rem transigere. mea intercessio et est et fuit parata. 2. nos hic incredibili ac singulari populi voluntate de C. Macro transegimus. cui quum aequi fuissemus, tamen multo maiorem fructum ex populi existimatione illo damnato cepimus quam ex ipsius, si absolutus esset, gratia cepissemus. 3. quod ad me de Hermathena scribis, per mihi gratum est ornamentum, et Academiae proprium meae, quod Hermes commune omnium et Minerva singulare est insigne eius gymnasii. qua re velim, ut scribis, caeteris quoque rebus quam plurimis eum locum ornes.

quae mihi antea signa misisti, ea nondum vidi. in Formiano sunt, quo ego nunc proficisci cogitabam. illa omnia in Tusculanum deportabo. Caietam, si quando abundare coepero, ornabo. libros tuos conserva et noli desperare eos me meos facere posse. quod si adsequor, supero Crassum divitiis atque omnium vicos et prata contemno.

.V.

(*Romae. Metello, Marcio coss.* 686.)

CICERO ATTICO S.

1. Quantum dolorem acceperim et quanto fructu sim privatus et forensi et domestico Lucii fratris nostri morte, in primis pro nostra consuetudine tu existimare potes. nam mihi omnia, quae iucunda ex humanitate alterius et moribus homini accidere possunt, ex illo accidebant. qua re non dubito quin tibi quoque id molestum sit, quum et meo dolore moveare et ipse omni virtute officioque ornatissimum tuique et sua sponte et meo sermone amantem adfinem amicumque amiseris. 2. quod ad me scribis de sorore tua, testis erit tibi ipsa quantae mihi curae fuerit, ut Quinti fratris animus in eam esset is qui esse deberet. quem quum esse offensiorem arbitrarer, eas litteras ad eum misi, quibus et placarem ut fratrem et monerem ut minorem et obiurgarem ut errantem. itaque ex iis, quae postea saepe ab eo ad me scripta sunt, confido ita esse omnia, ut et oporteat et velimus. 3. de litterarum missione sine causa abs te accusor. nunquam enim a Pomponia nostra certior sum factus

esse cui dare litteras possem: porro autem neque mihi accidit ut haberem qui in Epirum proficisceretur, neque dum te Athenis esse audiebamus. 4. de Acutiliano autem negocio quod mihi mandaras, ut primum a tuo digressu Romam veni, confeceram, sed accidit ut et contentione nihil opus esset et ut ego, qui in te satis consilii statuerim esse, mallem Peducaeum tibi consilium per litteras quam me dare. etenim quum multos dies aures meas Acutilio dedissem, cuius sermonis genus tibi notum esse arbitror, non mihi grave duxissem scribere ad te de illius querimoniis, quum eas audire, quod erat subodiosum, leve putassem. sed abs te ipso, qui me accusas, unas mihi scito litteras redditas esse, quum et ocii ad scribendum plus et facultatem dandi maiorem habueris. 5. quod scribis, etiam si cuius animus in te esset offensior, a me recolligi oportere, [teneo] quid dicas, neque id neglexi, sed est miro quodam modo adfectus. ego autem, quae dicenda fuerunt de te, non praeterii: quid autem contendendum esset ex tua putabam voluntate statuere oportere: quam si ad me perscripseris, intelliges me neque diligentiorem esse voluisse quam tu esses, neque negligentiorem fore quam tu velis. 6. de Tadiana re, mecum Tadius locutus est te ita scripsisse, nihil esse iam quod laboraretur, quoniam hereditas usu capta esset. id mirabamur te ignorare, de tutela legitima, in qua dicitur esse puella, nihil usu capi posse. 7. Epiroticam emptionem gaudeo tibi placere. quae tibi mandavi et quae tu intelliges convenire nostro Tusculano, velim, ut scribis, cures, quod sine molestia tua facere poteris. nam nos ex omnibus molestiis et laboribus uno illo in loco conquiescimus. 8. Quintum fratrem cotidie exspectamus. Terentia magnos articulorum dolores habet, et te et sororem tuam et matrem maxime diligit, salutemque tibi plurimam ascribit et Tulliola, deliciae nostrae. cura ut valeas et nos ames et tibi persuadeas te a me fraterne amari.

VI.

(Romae. Metello, Marcio coss. 686.)

Cicero Attico S.

1. Non committam posthac ut me accusare de epistolarum negligentia possis. tu modo videto in tanto ocio ut par mihi sis. domum Rabirianam Neapoli, quam tu iam dimensam et exaedificatam animo habebas, M'. Fonteius emit HS CCCIƆƆ XXX, id te scire volui, si quid forte ea res ad cogitationes tuas pertineret. 2. Quintus frater, ut mihi videtur, quo volumus animo est in Pomponiam, et cum ea nunc in Arpinatibus praediis erat et secum habebat hominem χρηστομαθῆ, D. Turranium. pater nobis discessit a. d. VIII Kal. Decembres. haec habebam fere quae te scire vellem. tu velim, si qua ornamenta γυμνασιώδη reperire poteris, quae loci sint eius quem tu non ignoras, ne praetermittas. nos Tusculano ita delectamur, ut nobismet ipsis tum denique, quum illo venimus, placeamus. quid agas omnibus de rebus et quid acturus sis fac nos quam diligentissime certiores.

VII.

(Romae. Metello, Marcio coss. 686.)

Cicero Attico S.

Apud matrem recte est, eaque nobis curae est. L. Cincio HS XXCD constitui me curaturum Idibus Februariis. tu velim ea, quae nobis emisse et parasse scribis, des operam ut quam primum habeamus, et velim cogites, id quod mihi pollicitus es, quem ad modum bibliothecam nobis conficere possis. omnem spem˙ delectationis nostrae, quam, quum in ocium venerimus, habere volumus, in tua humanitate positam habemus.

VIII.

(Romae. Pisone, Glabrione coss. 687.)

Cicero Attico S.

1. Apud te est, ut volumus. mater tua et soror a me Quintoque fratre diligitur. cum Acutilio sum locutus. is sibi negat a suo procuratore quidquam scriptum esse, et miratur istam controversiam fuisse quod ille recusaret satis dare amplius abs te non peti. quod te de Tadiano negocio decidisse scribis, id ego Tadio et gratum esse intellexi et magno opere iucundum. ille noster amicus, vir mehercule optimus et mihi amicissimus, sane tibi iratus est. hoc si quanti tu aestimes sciam, tum quid mihi elaborandum sit scire possim. 2. L. Cincio HS CCIƆƆ CCIƆƆ CCCC pro signis Megaricis, ut tu ad me scripseras, curavi. Hermae tui Pentelici

cum capitibus aëncis, de quibus ad me scripsisti,
iam nunc me admodum delectant. qua re velim
et eos et signa et caetera, quae tibi eius loci et
nostri studii et tuae elegantiae esse videbuntur,
quam plurima quam primumque mittas, et maxime
quae tibi gymnasii xystique videbuntur esse. nam
in eo genere sic studio efferimur, ut abs te adiu-
vandi, ab aliis prope reprehendendi simus. si Len-
tuli navis non erit, quo tibi placebit imponito. Tulliola, deliciolae nostrae, tuum munusculum flagitat
et me ut sponsorem appellat. mihi autem abiurare
certius est quam dependere.

IX.

(*Romae. Pisone, Glabrione coss.* 687.)

CICERO ATTICO S.

1. Nimium raro nobis abs te litterae adferun-
tur, quum et multo tu facilius reperias qui Romam
proficiscantur quam ego qui Athenas, et certius tibi
sit me esse Romae quam mihi te Athenis. itaque
propter hanc dubitationem meam brevior haec ipsa
epistola est, quod, quum incertus essem ubi esses,
nolebam illum nostrum familiarem sermonem in
alienas manus devenire. 2. signa Megarica et
Hermas, de quibus ad me scripsisti, vehementer
exspecto. quidquid eiusdem generis habebis, dig-
num Academia tibi quod videbitur, ne dubitaris mittere, et arcae nostrae confidito. genus hoc est
voluptatis meae: quae γυμνασιώδη maxime sunt,
ea quaero. Lentulus naves suas pollicetur. peto
abs te, ut haec cures diligenter. Chilius te rogat
et ego eius rogatu Εὐμολπιδῶν πάτρια.

X.

(In Tusculano. Pisone, Glabrione coss. 687.)
Cicero Attico S.

1. Quum essem in Tusculano—erit hoc tibi pro illo tuo *quum essem in Ceramico*—verum tamen quum ibi essem, Roma puer a sorore tua missus epistolam mihi abs te adlatam dedit nunciavitque eo ipso die post meridiem iturum eum, qui ad te proficisceretur. eo factum est, ut epistolae tuae rescriberem aliquid, brevitate temporis tam pauca cogerer scribere. 2. primum tibi de nostro amico placando aut etiam plane restituendo polliceor. quod ego etsi mea sponte ante faciebam, eo nunc tamen et agam studiosius et contendam ab illo vehementius, quod tantam ex epistola voluntatem eius rei tuam perspicere videor. hoc te intelligere volo, pergraviter illum esse offensum, sed quia nullam video gravem subesse causam magno opere confido illum fore in officio et in nostra potestate. 3. signa nostra et Hermeraclas, ut scribis, quum commodissime poteris, velim imponas, et si quod aliud οἰκεῖον eius loci, quem non ignoras, reperies, et maxime quae tibi palaestrae gymnasiique videbuntur esse. etenim ibi sedens haec ad te scribebam, ut me locus ipse admoneret. praeterea typos tibi mando, quos in tectorio atrioli possim includere, et putealia sigillata duo. 4. bibliothecam tuam cave cuiquam despondeas, quamvis acrem amatorem inveneris: nam ego omnes meas vindemiolas eo reservo, ut illud subsidium senectuti parem. 5. de fratre confido ita esse, ut semper volui et elaboravi.

multa signa sunt eius rei, non minimum, quod soror praegnans est. 6. de comitiis meis et tibi me permisisse memini et ego iam pridem hoc communibus amicis, qui te exspectant, praedico: te non modo non arcessi a me, sed prohiberi, quod intelligam multo magis interesse tua te agere quod agendum est hoc tempore quam mea te adesse comitiis. proinde eo animo te velim esse, quasi mei negocii causa in ista loca missus esses. me autem eum et offendes erga te et audies, quasi mihi, si quae parta erunt, non modo te praesente sed per te parta sint. Tulliola tibi diem dat, sponsorem appellat.

XI.

(Romae. Pisone, Glabrione coss. 687.)

CICERO ATTICO S.

1. Et mea sponte faciebam antea et post duabus epistolis tuis perdiligenter in eamdem rationem scriptis magno opere sum commotus. eo accedebat hortator adsiduus Sallustius, ut agerem quam diligentissime cum Lucceio de vestra vetere gratia reconcilianda. sed, quum omnia fecissem, non modo eam voluntatem eius quae fuerat erga te recuperare non potui, verum ne causam quidem elicere immutatae voluntatis. tametsi iactat ille quidem illud tuum arbitrium et ea quae iam tum quum aderas offendere eius animum intelligebam, tamen habet quiddam profecto quod magis in animo eius insederit, quod neque epistolae tuae neque nostra adlegatio tam potest facile delere, quam tu praesens non modo oratione sed tuo vultu illo familiari tolles,

si modo tanti putaris: id quod, si me audies et si humanitati tuae constare voles, certe putabis. ac ne illud mirere, cur, quum ego antea significarem tibi per litteras me sperare illum in nostra potestate fore, nunc idem videar diffidere, incredibile est quanto mihi videatur illius voluntas obstinatior et in hac iracundia obfirmatior: sed haec aut sanabuntur quum veneris, aut ei molesta erunt in utro culpa erit. 2. quod in epistola tua scriptum erat, me iam arbitrari designatum esse: scito nihil tam exercitum esse nunc Romae quam candidatos omnibus iniquitatibus nec quando futura sint comitia sciri. verum haec audies de Philadelpho. 3. tu velim quae Academiae nostrae parasti quam primum mittas. mire quam illius loci non modo usus, sed etiam cogitatio delectat. libros vero tuos cave cuiquam tradas. nobis eos, quem ad modum scribis, conserva. summum me eorum studium tenet, sicut odium iam caeterarum rerum: quas tu incredibile est quam brevi tempore quanto deteriores offensurus sis quam reliquisti.

XII.

(Romae. Messala, Pisone coss. 693.)

CICERO ATTICO S.

1. Τεῦκρις illa lentum sane negocium, neque Cornelius ad Terentiam postea rediit: opinor, ad Considium, Axium, Selicium confugiendum est, nam a Caecilio propinqui minore centesimis numum movere non possunt. sed, ut ad prima illa redeam, nihil ego illa impudentius, astutius, lentius vidi: *libertum mitto: Tito mandavi:* σκήψεις atque ἀνα-

βολαί. sed nescio an ταὐτόματον ἡμῶν· nam mihi Pompeiani πρόδρομοι nunciant aperte Pompeium acturum Antonio succedi oportere, eodemque tempore aget praetor ad populum. res eius modi est, ut ego nec per bonorum nec popularem existimationem honeste possim hominem defendere, nec mihi libeat, quod vel maximum est. etenim accidit hoc, quod totum cuius modi sit mando tibi ut perspicias. 2. libertum ego habeo, sane nequam hominem, Hilarum dico, ratiocinatorem et clientem tuum. de eo mihi Valerius interpres nunciat Chiliusque se audisse scribit haec: esse hominem cum Antonio: Antonium porro in cogendis pecuniis dictitare partem mihi quaeri, et a me custodem communis quaestus libertum esse missum. non sum mediocriter commotus neque tamen credidi, sed certe aliquid sermonis fuit. totum investiga, cognosce, perspice, et nebulonem illum, si quo pacto potes, ex istis locis amove. huius sermonis Valerius auctorem Cn. Plancium nominabat. mando tibi plane totum ut videas cuius modi sit. 3. Pompeium nobis amicissimum constat esse. divortium Muciae vehementer probatur. P. Clodium, Appii F., credo te audisse cum veste muliebri deprehensum domi C. Caesaris, quum pro populo fieret, cumque per manus servulae servatum et eductum: rem esse insigni infamia: quod te moleste ferre certo scio. 4. quid praeterea ad te scribam non habeo. et mehercule eram in scribendo conturbatior. nam puer festivus, ἀναγνώστης noster, Sositheus decesserat meque plus, quam servi mors debere videbatur, commoverat. tu velim saepe ad nos scribas. si rem nullam habebis, quod in buccam venerit scribito. Kal. Ianuar. M. Messala M. Pisone coss.

XIII.
(Romae. Messala, Pisone coss. 693.)
Cicero Attico S.

1. Accepi tuas tres iam epistolas: unam a M. Cornelio, quam Tribus Tabernis, ut opinor, ei dedisti: alteram, quam mihi Canusinus tuus hospes reddidit: tertiam, quam, ut scribis, ancoris sublatis de phaselo dedisti: quae fuerunt omnes † rhetorum. pure loquuntur, quum humanitatis sparsae sale tum insignes amoris notis. quibus epistolis sum equidem abs te lacessitus ad scribendum, sed idcirco sum tardior, quod non invenio fidelem tabellarium. quotus enim quisque est qui epistolam paullo graviorem ferre possit, nisi eam pellectione relevarit? accedit eo, quod mihi non ..... est, ut quisque in Epirum proficiscitur. ego enim te arbitror, caesis apud Amaltheam tuam victimis, statim esse ad Sicyonem oppugnandum profectum. neque tamen id ipsum certum habeo quando ad Antonium proficiscare aut quid in Epiro temporis ponas. ita neque Achaicis hominibus neque Epiroticis paullo liberiores litteras committere audeo. 2. sunt autem post discessum a me tuum res dignae litteris nostris, sed non committendae eius modi periculo ut aut interire aut aperiri aut intercipi possint. primum igitur scito primum me non esse rogatum sententiam praepositumque esse nobis pacificatorem Allobrogum, idque admurmurante senatu neque me invito esse factum. sum enim et ab observando homine

perverso liber et ad dignitatem in re publica retinendam contra illius voluntatem solutus, et ille secundus in dicendo locus habet auctoritatem paene principis et voluntatem non nimis devinctam beneficio consulis. tertius est Catulus, quartus, si etiam hoc quaeris, Hortensius. consul autem ipse parvo animo et pravo, tantum cavillator genere illo moroso quod etiam sine dicacitate ridetur, facie magis quam facetiis ridiculus, nihil agens cum re publica, sciunctus ab optimatibus, a quo nihil speres boni rei publicae, quia non vult, nihil [metuas] mali, quia non audet. eius autem collega et in me perhonorificus et partium studiosus ac defensor bonarum. quin imo leviter inter se dissident. 3. sed vereor ne hoc, quod infectum est, serpat longius. credo enim te audisse, quum apud Caesarem pro populo fieret, venisse eo muliebri vestitu virum, idque sacrificium quum virgines instaurassent, mentionem a Q. Cornificio in senatu factam—is fuit princeps, ne tu forte aliquem nostrum putes—postea rem ex senatus consulto ad pontifices relatam idque ab iis nefas esse decretum : deinde ex senatus consulto consules rogationem promulgasse : uxori Caesarem nuncium remisisse. in hac causa Piso amicitia P. Clodii ductus operam dat ut ea rogatio, quam ipse fert et fert ex senatus consulto et de religione, antiquetur. Messala vehementer adhuc agit severe. boni viri precibus Clodii removentur a causa : operae comparantur: nosmet ipsi, qui Lycurgei a principio fuissemus, cotidie demitigamur: instat et urget Cato. quid multa ? vereor ne haec neglecta a bonis, defensa ab improbis, magnorum rei publicae malorum causa sit. 4. tuus autem ille

amicus—scin quem dicam?—de quo tu ad me
scripsisti, postea quam non auderet reprehendere,
laudare coepisse, nos, ut ostendit, admodum diligit,
amplectitur, amat, aperte laudat: occulte, sed ita
ut perspicuum sit, invidet. nihil come, nihil
simplex, nihil ἐν τοῖς πολιτικοῖς honestum, nihil
illustre, nihil forte, nihil liberum. sed haec ad te
scribam alias subtilius: nam neque adhuc mihi
satis nota sunt et huic terrae filio nescio cui committere epistolam tantis de rebus non audeo. 5.
provincias praetores nondum sortiti sunt. res eodem
est loci, quo reliquisti. Τοποθεσίαν quam postu-
las Miseni et Puteolorum includam orationi meae.
a. d. III Non. Decembr. mendose fuisse animad-
verteram. quae laudas ex orationibus, mihi crede,
valde mihi placebant, sed non audebam antea
dicere: nunc vero, quod a te probata sunt, multo
mihi ἀττικώτερα videntur. in illam orationem Metellinam addidi quaedam. liber tibi mittetur, quoniam te amor nostri φιλορήτορα reddidit. 6. novi
tibi quidnam scribam? quid? etiam. Messala consul Autronianam domum emit HS. XXXVII. quid
id ad me, inquies? tantum, quod ea emptione et
nos bene emisse iudicati sumus et homines intelligere coeperunt licere amicorum facultatibus in
emendo ad dignitatem aliquam pervenire. Τεῦκρις
illa lentum negocium est, sed tamen est in spe.
tu ista confice. a nobis liberiorem epistolam exspecta. VI Kalend. Febr. M. Messala M. Pisone
coss.

XIV.

(Romae. Messala, Pisone coss. 693.)

Cicero Attico S.

1. Vereor ne putidum sit scribere ad te quam sim occupatus, sed tamen distinebar, ut huic vix tantulae epistolae tempus habuerim atque id ereptum e summis occupationibus. prima contio Pompeii qualis fuisset scripsi ad te antea, non iucunda miseris, inanis improbis, beatis non grata, bonis non gravis, itaque frigebat. tum Pisonis consulis impulsu levissimus tribunus plebis Fufius in contionem produxit Pompeium. res agebatur in circo Flaminio et erat in eo ipso loco illo die nundinarum πανήγυρις. quaesivit ex eo placeretne ei iudices a praetore legi, quo consilio idem praetor uteretur. id autem erat de Clodiana religione ab senatu constitutum. 2. tum Pompeius μάλ' ἀριστοκρατικῶς locutus est, senatusque auctoritatem sibi omnibus in rebus maximam videri semperque visam esse respondit et id multis verbis. postea Messala consul in senatu de Pompeio quaesivit quid de religione et de promulgata rogatione sentiret. locutus ita est in senatu, ut omnia illius ordinis consulta γενικῶς laudaret, mihique, ut adsedit, dixit se putare satis ab se etiam de istis rebus esse responsum. 3. Crassus postea quam vidit illum excepisse laudem ex eo quod suspicarentur homines ei consulatum meum placere, surrexit ornatissimeque de meo consulatu locutus est, ut ita diceret, se, quod esset senator, quod civis, quod liber, quod viveret, mihi acceptum referre: quotiens coniugem,

quotiens domum, quotiens patriam videret, totiens se beneficium meum videre. quid multa? totum hunc locum, quem ego varie meis orationibus, quarum tu Aristarchus es, soleo pingere, de flamma, de ferro—nosti illas ληκύθους—, valde graviter pertexuit. proxime Pompeium sedebam. intellexi hominem moveri, utrum Crassum inire eam gratiam, quam ipse praetermisisset, an esse tantas res nostras, quae tam libenti senatu laudarentur, ab eo praesertim, qui mihi laudem illam eo minus deberet, quod meis omnibus litteris in Pompeiana laude perstrictus esset. 4. hic dies me valde Crasso adiunxit, et tamen ab illo aperte tecte quidquid est datum libenter accepi. ego autem ipse, di boni! quo modo ἐνεπερπερευσάμην novo auditori Pompeio! si umquam mihi περίοδοι ἢ καμπαὶ ἢ ἐνθυμήματα ἢ κατασκευαὶ suppeditaverunt, illo tempore. quid multa? clamores. etenim haec erat ὑπόθεσις, de gravitate ordinis, de equestri concordia, de consensione Italiae, de intermortuis reliquiis coniurationis, de vilitate, de ocio. nosti iam in hac materia sonitus nostros: tanti fuerunt, ut ego eo brevior sim, quod eos usque istim exauditos putem. 5. Romanae autem se res sic habent: senatus Ἄρειος πάγος. nihil constantius, nihil severius, nihil fortius. nam, quum dies venisset rogationi ex senatus consulto ferendae, concursabant barbatuli iuvenes, totus ille grex Catilinae, duce filiola Curionis, et populum, ut antiquaret, rogabant. Piso autem consul, lator rogationis, idem erat dissuasor. operae Clodianae pontes occuparant: tabellae ministrabantur ita ut nulla daretur UTI ROGAS. hic tibi rostra Cato advolat, convicium Pisoni consuli mirificum facit, si id est convicium, vox plena gravitatis, plena auctoritatis, plena denique salutis. accedit eodem etiam noster Hortensius, multi praeterea boni. insignis vero opera Favonii fuit. hoc concursu optimatum comitia dimittuntur: senatus vocatur. quum decerneretur frequenti senatu, contra pugnante Pisone, ad pedes omnium singillatim accidente Clodio, ut consules populum cohortarentur ad rogationem accipiendam, homines ad XV Curioni nullum senatus consultum facienti adsenserunt: ex altera parte facile CCCC fuerunt. acta res est. Fufius tribunus tum concessit. Clodius contiones miseras habebat, in quibus Lucullum, Hortensium, C. Pisonem, Messalam consulem contumeliose laedebat: me tantum *comperisse omnia* criminabatur. senatus et de provinciis praetorum et de legationibus et de caeteris rebus decernebat, ut ante quam rogatio lata esset ne quid ageretur. 6. habes res Romanas, sed tamen etiam illud, quod non speraram, audi. Messala consul est egregius, fortis, constans, diligens, nostri laudator, amator, imitator. ille alter uno vitio minus vitiosus, quod iners, quod somni plenus, quod imperitus, quod ἀπρακτότατος, sed voluntate ita καχέκτης, ut Pompeium post illam contionem, in qua ab eo senatus laudatus est, odisse coeperit. itaque mirum in modum omnes a se bonos alienavit. neque id magis amicitia Clodii adductus facit quam studio perditarum rerum atque partium. sed habet sui similem in magistratibus praeter Fufium neminem. bonis utimur tribunis plebis, Cornuto vero Pseudocatone. quid quaeris? 7. nunc ut ad privata redeam, Τεῦκρις promissa patravit. tu mandata effice, quae recepisti. Quintus frater, qui Argiletani aedificii reliquum dodrantem emit HS DCCXXV, Tusculanum venditat, ut, si possit, emat Pacilianam domum. cum Lucceio in gratiam redi. video hominem valde petiturire. navabo operam. tu quid agas, ubi sis, cuius modi istac res sint fac me quam diligentissime certiorem. Idib. Febr.

XV.

(Romae. Messala, Pisone coss. 693.)

CICERO ATTICO S.

1. Asiam Quinto, suavissimo fratri, obtigisse audisti: non enim dubito quin celerius tibi hoc rumor quam ullius nostrum litterae nunciarint. nunc quoniam et laudis avidissimi semper fuimus, et practer caeteros φιλέλληνες et sumus et habemur, et multorum odia atque inimicitias rei publicae causa suscepimus, παντοίης ἀρετῆς μιμνήσκεο, curaque et effice ut ab omnibus et laudemur et amemur. 2. his de rebus plura ad te in ea epistola scribam, quam ipsi Quinto dabo. tu me velim certiorem facias quid de meis mandatis egeris, atque etiam quid de tuo negocio. nam ut Brundusio profectus es, nullae mihi abs te sunt redditae litterae. valde aveo scire quid agas. Idib. Mart.

XVI.

(Romae. Messala, Pisone coss. 693.)

CICERO ATTICO S.

1. Quaeris ex me quid acciderit de iudicio quod tam practer opinionem omnium factum sit,

et simul vis scire quo modo ego minus quam soleam proeliatus sim: respondebo tibi ὕστερον πρότερον, Ὁμηρικῶς. ego enim, quam diu senatus auctoritas mihi defendenda fuit, sic acriter et vehementer proeliatus sum, ut clamor concursusque maxima cum mea laude fierent. quod si tibi umquam sum visus in re publica fortis, certe me in illa causa admiratus esses. quum enim ille ad contiones confugisset in iisque meo nomine ad invidiam uteretur, di immortales! quas ego pugnas et quantas strages edidi! quos impetus in Pisonem, in Curionem, in totam illam manum feci! quo modo sum insectatus levitatem senum, libidinem iuventutis! saepe, ita me di iuvent! te non solum auctorem consiliorum meorum, verum etiam spectatorem pugnarum mirificarum desideravi. 2. postea vero quam Hortensius excogitavit, ut legem de religione Fufius tribunus plebis ferret, in qua nihil aliud a consulari rogatione differebat nisi iudicum genus—in eo autem erant omnia—pugnavitque ut ita fieret, quod et sibi et aliis persuaserat nullis illum iudicibus effugere posse: contraxi vela perspiciens inopiam iudicum, neque dixi quidquam pro testimonio, nisi quod erat ita notum atque testatum, ut non possem praeterire. itaque si causam quaeris absolutionis, ut iam πρὸς τὸ πρότερον revertar, egestas iudicum fuit et turpitudo. id autem ut accideret, commissum est Hortensii consilio, qui dum veritus est ne Fufius ei legi intercederet, quae ex senatus consulto ferebatur, non vidit illud satius esse illum in infamia relinqui ac sordibus quam infirmo iudicio committi. sed ductus odio properavit rem deducere in iudicium, quum

illum plumbeo gladio iugulatum iri tamen diceret.
3. sed iudicium si quaeris quale fuerit, incredibili
exitu: sic uti nunc ex eventu ab aliis, a me tamen
ex ipso initio, consilium Hortensii reprehendatur.
nam ut reiectio facta est clamoribus maximis,
quum accusator tamquam censor bonus homines
nequissimos reiiceret, reus tamquam clemens lanista frugalissimum quemque secerneret, ut primum
iudices consederunt, valde diffidere boni coeperunt.
non enim umquam turpior in ludo talario consessus
fuit. maculosi senatores, nudi equites, tribuni non
tam aerati quam, ut appellantur, aerarii. pauci
tamen boni inerant, quos reiectione fugare ille non
potuerat, qui maesti inter sui dissimiles et maeren-
tes sedebant et contagione turpitudinis vehementer
permovebantur. 4. hic, ut quaeque res ad consilium primis postulationibus referebatur, incredi-
bilis erat severitas nulla varietate sententiarum,
nihil impetrabat reus, plus accusatori dabatur quam
postulabat, triumphabat—quid quaeris?—Hortensius se vidisse tantum, nemo erat qui illum reum
ac non miliens condemnatum arbitraretur. me vero
teste producto credo te ex acclamatione Clodii
advocatorum audisse quae consurrectio iudicum
facta sit, ut me circumsteterint, ut aperte iugula
sua pro meo capite P. Clodio ostentarint. quae
mihi res multo honorificentior visa est quam aut
illa, quum iurare tui cives Xenocratem testimonium dicentem prohibuerunt, aut quum tabulas
Metelli Numidici, quum eae, ut mos est, circum-
ferrentur, nostri iudices aspicere noluerunt: multo
haec, inquam, nostra res maior. 5. itaque iudicum
vocibus, quum ego sic ab iis ut salus patriae defen-

derer, fractus reus et una patroni omnes conciderunt. ad me autem eadem frequentia postridie convenit, quacum abiens consulatu sum domum reductus. clamare praeclari Areopagitae se non esse venturos nisi praesidio constituto. refertur ad consilium: una sola sententia praesidium non desideravit. defertur res ad senatum: gravissime ornatissimeque decernitur: laudantur iudices: datur negocium magistratibus: responsurum hominem nemo arbitrabatur.

Ἔσπετε νῦν μοι, Μοῦσαι,—
ὅππως δὴ πρῶτον πῦρ ἔμπεσε.

nosti Calvum, ex Nanneianis illum, illum laudatorem meum, de cuius oratione erga me honorifica ad te scripseram. biduo per unum servum et eum ex gladiatorio ludo confecit totum negocium: arcessivit ad se, promisit, intercessit, dedit. iam vero—o di boni, rem perditam!—etiam noctes certarum mulierum atque adolescentulorum nobilium introductiones non nullis iudicibus pro mercedis cumulo fuerunt. ita, summo discessu bonorum, pleno foro servorum, XXV iudices ita fortes tamen fuerunt, ut, summo proposito periculo, vel perire maluerint quam perdere omnia: XXXI fuerunt quos fames magis quam fama commoverit. quorum Catulus quum vidisset quemdam: quid vos, inquit, praesidium a nobis postulabatis? an ne numi vobis eriperentur timebatis? 6. habes, ut brevissime potui, genus iudicii et causam absolutionis. quaeris deinceps qui nunc sit status rerum et qui meus. rei publicae statum illum, quem tu meo consilio, ego divino confirmatum putabam, qui bonorum omnium coniunctione et auctoritate consulatus mei fixus et fundatus videbatur, nisi qui nos deus respexerit, elapsum scito esse de manibus uno hoc iudicio: si iudicium est, triginta homines populi Romani levissimos ac nequissimos numulis acceptis ius ac fas omne delere et, quod omnes non modo homines verum etiam pecudes factum esse sciant, id Thalnam et Plautum et Spongiam et caeteras huius modi quisquilias statuere numquam esse factum. 7. sed tamen, ut te de re publica consoler, non ita, ut sperarunt mali, tanto imposito rei publicae vulnere, alacris exsultat improbitas in victoria. nam plane ita putaverunt, quum religio, quum pudicitia, quum iudiciorum fides, quum senatus auctoritas concidisset, fore ut aperte victrix nequitia ac libido poenas ab optimo quoque peteret sui doloris, quem improbissimo cuique inusserat severitas consulatus mei. 8. idem ego ille—non enim mihi videor insolenter gloriari, quum de me apud te loquor, in ea praesertim epistola quam nolo ab aliis legi— idem, inquam, ego recreavi adflictos animos bonorum, unum quemque confirmans, excitans: insectandis vero exagitandisque numariis iudicibus omnem omnibus studiosis ac fautoribus illius victoriae παῤῥησίαν eripui, Pisonem consulem nulla in re consistere umquam sum passus, desponsam homini iam Syriam ademi, senatum ad pristinam suam severitatem revocavi atque abiectum excitavi, Clodium praesentem fregi in senatu quum oratione perpetua, plenissima gravitatis, tum altercatione eius modi, ex qua licet pauca degustes. nam caetera non possunt habere neque vim neque venustatem, remoto illo studio contentionis, quem ἀγῶνα vos appellatis. 9. nam, ut Idib. Maiis in senatum convenimus, rogatus ego sententiam multa dixi de summa re publica, atque ille locus inductus a me est divinitus: ne una plaga accepta patres conscripti conciderent, ne deficerent: vulnus esse eius modi, quod mihi nec dissimulandum nec pertimescendum videretur, ne aut metuendo ignavissimi aut ignorando stultissimi iudicaremur: bis absolutum esse Lentulum, bis Catilinam, hunc tertium iam esse a iudicibus in rem publicam immissum. erras, Clodi: non te iudices urbi, sed carceri reservarunt, neque te retinere in civitate, sed exsilio privare voluerunt. quam ob rem, patres conscripti, erigite animos, retinete vestram dignitatem. manet illa in re publica bonorum consensio: dolor accessit bonis viris, virtus non est imminuta: nihil est damni factum novi, sed, quod erat, inventum est. in unius hominis perditi iudicio plures similes reperti sunt. 10. sed quid ago? paene orationem in epistolam inclusi. redeo ad altercationem. surgit pulchellus puer, obiicit mihi *me ad Baias fuisse.* falsum, sed tamen quid hoc? simile est, inquam, quasi dicas in operto fuisse. *quid,* inquit, *homini Arpinati cum aquis calidis?* narra, inquam, patrono tuo, qui Arpinatis aquas concupivit. (nosti enim Marianas.) *quousque,* inquit, *hunc regem feremus?* regem appellas, inquam, quum Rex tui mentionem nullam fecerit? (ille autem Regis hereditatem spe devorarat.) *domum,* inquit, *emisti.* potes, inquam, dicere, 'iudices emisti'? *iuranti,* inquit, *tibi non crediderunt.* mihi vero, inquam, XXV iudices crediderunt, XXXI, quoniam numos ante acceperunt, tibi nihil crediderunt. magnis clamoribus adflictus conticuit et concidit. 11. noster autem status est hic: apud bonos iidem sumus, quos reliquisti, apud sordem urbis et faecem multo melius nunc, quam reliquisti. nam et illud nobis non obest, videri nostrum testimonium non valuisse—missus est sanguis invidiae sine dolore—atque etiam hoc magis, quod omnes illi fautores illius flagitii rem manifestam illam redemptam esse a iudicibus confitentur: accedit, quod illa contionalis hirudo aerarii, misera ac ieiuna plebecula, me ab hoc Magno unice diligi putat, et hercule multa et iucunda consuetudine coniuncti inter nos sumus, usque eo, ut nostri isti comissatores coniurationis, barbatuli iuvenes, illum in sermonibus Cnaeum Ciceronem appellent. itaque et ludis et gladiatoribus mirandas ἐπισημασίας sine ulla pastoricia fistula auferebamus. 12. nunc est exspectatio ingens comitiorum, in quae omnibus invitis trudit noster Magnus Auli filium, atque in eo neque auctoritate neque gratia pugnat, sed quibus Philippus omnia castella expugnari posse dicebat, in quae modo asellus onustus auro posset ascendere. consul autem ille, Doterionis histrionis similis, suscepisse negocium dicitur et domi divisores habere: quod ego non credo. sed senatus consulta duo iam facta sunt, odiosa, quod in consulem facta putantur, Catone et Domitio postulante, unum, ut apud magistratus inquiri liceret, alterum, cuius domi divisores habitarent, adversus rem publicam. 13. Lurco autem tribunus plebis [est], qui, magistratum simul † contra legem Aeliam iniit, solutus est et Aelia et Fufia ut legem de ambitu ferret, quam ille bono auspicio claudus homo promulgavit. ita comitia in ante diem VI Kal. Sext. dilata sunt. novi est in lege

hoc, ut, qui númos in tribus pronunciarit, si non
dederit, impune sit: sin dederit, ut quoad vivat
singulis tribubus HS CIϽ CIϽ CIϽ debeat. dixi
hanc legem P. Clodium iam ante servasse: pronunciare enim solitum esse et non dare. sed heus tu!
videsne consulatum illum nostrum, quem Curio
antea ἀποθέωσιν vocabat, si hic factus erit, fabulam
mimum futurum? qua re, ut opinor, φιλοσοφητέον,
id quod tu facis, et istos consulatus non flocci
facteon. 14. quod ad me scribis, te in Asiam
statuisse non ire, equidem mallem ut ires, ac vereor
ne quid in ista re minus commode fiat. sed tamen
non possum reprehendere consilium tuum, praesertim quum egomet in provinciam non sim profectus. 15. epigrammatis tuis, quae in Amaltheo
posuisti, contenti erimus, praesertim quum et
Chilius nos reliquerit et Archias nihil de me
scripserit, ac vereor ne, Lucullis quoniam Graecum
poëma condidit, nunc ad Caecilianam fabulam
spectet. 16. Antonio tuo nomine gratias egi, cam-
que epistolam Manlio dedi. ad te ideo antea
rarius scripsi, quod non habebam idoneum cui
darem nec satis sciebam quo darem. valde te
vindicavi. 17. Cincius si quid ad me tui negocii
detulerit, suscipiam. sed nunc magis in suo est
occupatus, in quo ego ei non desum. tu, si uno in
loco es futurus, crebras a nobis litteras exspecta:
ast plures etiam ipse mittito. 18. velim ad me
scribas cuius modi sit ᾽Αμαλθεῖον tuum, quo ornatu,
qua τοποθεσίᾳ, et quae poëmata quasque historias
de ᾽Αμαλθείᾳ habes ad me mittas. lubet mihi facere
in Arpinati. ego tibi aliquid de meis scriptis mittam. nihil erat absoluti.

XVII.

(Romae. Messala, Pisone coss. 693.)

CICERO ATTICO S.

1. Magna mihi varietas voluntatis et dissimilitudo opinionis ac iudicii Quinti fratris mei demonstrata est ex litteris tuis, in quibus ad me epistolarum illius exempla misisti. qua ex re et molestia sum tanta adfectus, quantam mihi meus amor summus erga utrumque vestrum adferre debuit, et admiratione quidnam accidisset quod adferret Quinto fratri meo aut offensionem tam gravem aut commutationem tantam voluntatis. atque illud a me iam ante intelligebatur, quod te quoque ipsum discedentem a nobis suspicari videbam, subesse nescio quid opinionis incommodae sauciumque esse eius animum et insedisse quasdam odiosas suspiciones: quibus ego mederi quum cuperem antea saepe et vehementius etiam post sortitionem provinciae, nec tantum intelligebam ei esse offensionis, quantum litterae tuae declararant, nec tantum proficiebam, quantum volebam. 2. sed tamen hoc me ipse consolabar, quod non dubitabam quin te ille aut Dyrrhachii aut in istis locis uspiam visurus esset. quod quum accidisset, confidebam ac mihi persuaseram fore ut omnia placarentur inter vos non modo sermone ac disputatione, sed conspectu ipso congressuque vestro. nam quanta sit in Quinto fratre meo comitas, quanta iucunditas, quam mollis animus ad accipiendam et ad deponendam offensionem, nihil attinet me ad te, qui ea nosti, scribere. sed accidit perincom-

mode, quod eum nusquam vidisti. valuit enim plus, quod erat illi non nullorum artificiis inculcatum, quam aut officium aut necessitudo aut amor vester ille pristinus, qui plurimum valere debuit. 3. atque huius incommodi culpa ubi resideat facilius possum existimare quam scribere. vereor enim ne, dum defendam meos, non parcam tuis. nam sic intelligo, ut nihil a domesticis vulneris factum sit, illud quidem quod erat eos certe sanare potuisse. sed huiusce rei totius vitium, quod aliquanto etiam latius patet quam videtur, praesenti tibi commodius exponam. 4. de iis litteris, quas ad te Thessalonica misit, et de sermonibus, quos ab illo et Romae apud amicos tuos et in itinere habitos putas, ecquid tantum causae sit ignoro: sed omnis in tua posita est humanitate mihi spes huius levandae molestiae. nam, si ita statueris, et irritabiles animos esse optimorum saepe hominum et eosdem placabiles, et esse hanc agilitatem, ut ita dicam, mollitiamque naturae plerumque bonitatis et, id quod caput est, nobis inter nos nostra sive incommoda sive vitia sive iniurias esse tolerandas, facile haec, quem ad modum spero, mitigabuntur. quod ego ut facias te oro. nam ad me, qui te unice diligo, maxime pertinet neminem esse meorum, qui aut te non amet aut abs te non ametur. 5. illa pars epistolae tuae minime fuit necessaria, in qua exponis quas facultates aut provincialium aut urbanorum commodorum et aliis temporibus et me ipso consule praetermiseris. mihi enim perspecta est ingenuitas et magnitudo animi tui, neque ego inter me atque te quidquam interesse umquam duxi praeter voluntatem institutae vitae, quod me ambitio quaedam ad honorum studium, te autem alia minime reprehendenda ratio ad honestum ocium duxit. vera quidem laude probitatis, diligentiae, religionis neque me tibi neque quemquam antepono, amoris vero erga me, quum a fraterno amore domesticoque discessi, tibi primas defero. 6. vidi enim, vidi penitusque perspexi in meis variis temporibus et sollicitudines et laetitias tuas. fuit mihi saepe et laudis nostrae gratulatio tua iucunda et timoris consolatio grata. quin mihi nunc te absente non solum consilium, quo tu excellis, sed etiam sermonis communicatio, quae mihi suavissima tecum solet esse, maxime deest—quid dicam?—in publicane re, quo in genere mihi negligenti esse non licet, an in forensi labore, quem antea propter ambitionem sustinebam, nunc, ut dignitatem tueri gratia possim, an in ipsis domesticis negociis, in quibus ego quum antea tum vero post discessum fratris te sermonesque nostros desidero? postremo non labor meus, non requies, non negocium, non ocium, non forenses res, non domesticae, non publicae, non privatae carere diutius tuo suavissimo atque amantissimo consilio ac sermone possunt. 7. atque harum rerum commemorationem verecundia saepe impedivit utriusque nostrum. nunc autem ea fuit necessaria propter eam partem epistolae tuae, per quam te ac mores tuos mihi purgatos ac probatos esse voluisti. atque in ista incommoditate alienati illius animi et offensi illud inest tamen commodi, quod et mihi et caeteris amicis tuis nota fuit et abs te aliquando testificata tua voluntas omittendae provinciae, ut, quod una non estis, non dissensione ac discidio vestro, sed voluntate ac iudicio tuo factum esse videatur. qua re et illa, quae violata, expiabuntur et haec nostra, quae sunt sanctissime conservata, suam religionem obtinebunt. 8. nos hic in re publica infirma misera commutabilique versamur. credo enim te audisse nostros equites paene a senatu esse disiunctos: qui primum illud valde graviter tulerunt, promulgatum ex senatus consulto fuisse, ut de eis, qui ob iudicandum pecuniam accepissent, quaereretur. qua in re decernenda quum ego casu non adfuissem sensissemque id equestrem ordinem ferre moleste neque aperte dicere, obiurgavi senatum, ut mihi visus sum, summa cum auctoritate, et in causa non verecunda admodum gravis et copiosus fui. 9. ecce aliae deliciae equitum vix ferendae! quas ego non solum tuli, sed etiam ornavi. Asiani, qui de censoribus conduxerunt, questi sunt in senatu se. cupiditate prolapsos nimium magno conduxisse: ut induceretur locatio, postulaverunt. ego princeps in adiutoribus atque adeo secundus. nam, ut illi auderent hoc postulare, Crassus eos impulit. invidiosa res, turpis postulatio et confessio temeritatis. summum erat periculum ne, si nihil impetrassent, plane alienarentur a senatu. huic quoque rei subventum est maxime a nobis perfectumque, ut frequentissimo senatu et libentissimo uterentur, multaque a me de ordinum dignitate et concordia dicta sunt Kal. Decembr. et postridie. neque adhuc res confecta est, sed voluntas senatus perspecta. unus enim contra dixerat Metellus consul designatus. quin erat dicturus — ad quem propter diei brevitatem perventum non est — heros ille noster Cato. 10. sic ego conservans rationem institutionemque nostram tueor, ut possum, illam a me conglutinatam concordiam, sed tamen, quoniam ista sunt infirma, munitur quaedam nobis ad retinendas opes nostras tuta, ut spero, via, quam tibi litteris satis explicare non possum, significatione parva ostendam tamen. utor Pompeio familiarissime. video quid dicas. cavebo quae sunt cavenda ac scribam alias ad te de meis consiliis capessendae rei publicae plura. 11. Lucceium scito consulatum habere in animo statim petere: duo enim soli dicuntur petituri. Caesar cum eo coire per Arrium cogitat et Bibulus cum hoc se putat per C. Pisonem posse coniungi. rides? non sunt haec ridicula, mihi crede. quid aliud scribam ad te? quid? multa sunt, sed in aliud tempus. te si exspectari velis, cures ut sciam. iam illud modeste rogo, quod maxime cupio, ut quam primum venias. Nonis Decembribus.

XVIII.

(Romae. Metello, Afranio coss. 694.)

CICERO ATTICO S.

1. Nihil mihi nunc scito tam deesse quam hominem eum, quicum omnia, quae me cura aliqua adficiunt, una communicem: qui me amet, qui sapiat, quicum ego colloquar, nihil fingam, nihil dissimulem, nihil obtegam. abest enim frater ἀφελέστατος et amantissimus [mei]. en tellus! non homo, sed
littus atque aër et solitudo mera!
tu autem, qui saepissime curam et angorem animi mei sermone et consilio levasti tuo, qui mihi et in

publica re socius et in privatis omnibus conscius et
omnium meorum sermonum et consiliorum particeps
esse soles, ubinam es? ita sum ab omnibus de-
stitutus, ut tantum requietis habeam, quantum cum
uxore et filiola et mellito Cicerone consumitur.
nam illae ambitiosae nostrae fucosaeque amicitiae
sunt in quodam splendore forensi, fructum domes-
ticum non habent. itaque, quum bene completa
domus est tempore matutino, quum ad forum sti-
pati gregibus amicorum descendimus, reperire ex
magna turba neminem possumus quicum aut iocari
libere aut suspirare familiariter possimus. qua
re te exspectamus, te desideramus, te iam etiam
arcessimus: multa sunt enim, quae me sollicitant
anguntque, quae mihi videor aures nactus tuas
unius ambulationis sermone exhaurire posse. 2.
ac domesticarum quidem sollicitudinum aculeos
omnes et scrupulos occultabo, neque ego huic epistolae atque ignoto tabellario committam. atque
hi — nolo enim te permoveri — non sunt permolesti,
sed tamen insident et urgent et nullius amantis
consilio aut sermone requiescunt. in re publica vero,
quamquam animus est praesens† et voluntas etiam,
tamen ea iam ipsa medicinam refugit. nam ut ea
breviter, quae post tuum discessum acta sunt, col-
ligam, iam exclames necesse est res Romanas diutius
stare non posse. etenim post profectionem tuam
primus, ut opinor, introitus fuit in causam fabulae
Clodianae, in qua ego nactus, ut mihi videbar,
locum resecandae libidinis et coërcendae iuventutis, vehemens fui et omnes profudi vires animi atque ingenii mei, non odio adductus alicuius, sed
spe rei publicae corrigendae et sanandae civitatis.

3. adflicta res publica est empto constupratoque iudicio. vide quae sint postea consecuta. consul est impositus is nobis, quem nemo praeter nos philosophos aspicere sine suspiritu posset. quantum hoc vulnus! facto senatus consulto de ambitu, de iudiciis, nulla lex perlata, exagitatus senatus, alienati equites Romani. sic ille annus duo firmamenta rei publicae per me unum constituta evertit: nam et senatus auctoritatem abiecit et ordinum concordiam disiunxit. instat hic nunc [ille] annus egregius. eius initium eius modi fuit, ut anniversaria sacra Iuventatis non committerentur. nam M. Luculli uxorem Memmius suis sacris initiavit. Menelaus aegre id passus divortium fecit. quamquam ille pastor Idaeus Menelaum solum contempserat, hic noster Paris tam Menelaum quam Agamemnonem liberum non putavit. 4. est autem C. Herennius quidam tribunus plebis, quem tu fortasse ne nosti quidem: tametsi potes nosse, tribulis enim tuus est et Sextus pater eius numos vobis dividere solebat: is ad plebem P. Clodium traducit, idemque fert, ut universus populus in campo Martio suffragium de re Clodii ferat. hunc ego accepi in senatu, ut soleo, sed nihil est illo homine lentius. 5. Metellus est consul egregius et nos amat, sed imminuit auctoritatem suam, quod habet dicis causa promulgatum illud † quidem de Clodio. Auli autem filius, o di immortales! quam ignavus ac sine animo miles! quam dignus, qui Palicano, sicut facit, os ad male audiendum cotidie praebeat! 6. Agraria autem promulgata est a Flavio, sane levis, eadem fere, quae fuit Plotia. sed interea πολιτικὸς ἀνὴρ οὐδ' ὄναρ quisquam inveniri potest.

qui poterat, familiaris noster—sic est enim: volo te hoc scire—Pompeius togulam illam pictam silentio tuetur suam. Crassus verbum nullum contra gratiam. caeteros iam nosti: qui ita sunt stulti, ut amissa re publica piscinas suas fore salvas sperare videantur. 7. unus est qui curet constantia magis et integritate quam, ut mihi videtur, consilio aut ingenio, Cato: qui miseros publicanos, quos habuit amantissimos sui, tertium iam mensem vexat, neque iis a senatu responsum dari patitur. Ita nos cogimur reliquis de rebus nihil decernere ante quam publicanis responsum sit. qua re etiam legationes reiectum iri puto. 8. nunc vides quibus fluctibus iactemur, et, si ex iis, quae scripsimus [tanta], etiam a me non scripta perspicis, revise nos aliquando et, quamquam sunt haec fugienda, quo te voco, tamen fac ut amorem nostrum tanti aestimes, ut eo vel cum his molestiis perfrui velis. nam, ne absens censeare, curabo edicendum et proponendum locis omnibus. sub lustrum autem censeri germani negociatoris est. qua re cura ut te quam primum videamus. vale. XI Kal. Febr. Q. Metello L. Afranio coss.

XIX.

(Romae. Metello, Afranio coss. 694.)

CICERO ATTICO S.

1. Non modo, si mihi tantum esset ocii, quantum est tibi, verum etiam, si tam breves epistolas vellem mittere, quam tu soles facere, te superarem et in scribendo multo essem crebrior quam tu. sed ad summas atque incredibiles occupationes meas accedit, quod nullam a me epistolam ad te sino

absque argumento ac sententia pervenire. et primum tibi ut aequum est civi amanti patriam, quae sunt in re publica, exponam: deinde, quoniam tibi amore nos proximi sumus, scribemus etiam de nobis ea, quae scire te non nolle arbitramur. 2. atque in re publica nunc quidem maxime Gallici belli versatur metus. nam Aedui, fratres nostri, pugnant, Sequani † permale pugnarunt, et Helvetii sine dubio sunt in armis excursionesque in provinciam faciunt. senatus decrevit, ut consules duas Gallias sortirentur, dilectus haberetur, vacationes ne valerent, legati cum auctoritate mitterentur qui adirent Galliae civitates darentque operam ne eae se cum Helvetiis coniungerent. legati sunt Q. Metellus Creticus et L. Flaccus et τὸ ἐπὶ τῇ φακῇ μύρον, Lentulus Clodiani filius. 3. atque hoc loco illud non queo praeterire, quod, quum de consularibus mea prima sors exisset, una voce senatus frequens retinendum me in urbe censuit. Hoc idem post me Pompeio accidit, ut nos duo quasi pignora rei publicae retineri videremur. quid enim ego aliorum in me ἐπιφωνήματα exspectem, quum haec domi nascantur? 4. urbanae autem res sic se habent. agraria lex a Flavio tribuno plebis vehementer agitabatur auctore Pompeio, quae nihil populare habebat praeter auctorem. ex hac ego lege secunda contionis voluntate omnia illa tollebam, quae ad privatorum incommodum pertinebant: liberabam agrum eum, qui P. Mucio L. Calpurnio consulibus publicus fuisset: Sullanorum hominum possessiones confirmabam: Volaterranos et Arretinos, quorum agrum Sulla publicarat neque diviserat, in sua possessione retinebam: unam rationem non reiiciebam, ut ager hac adventicia pecunia emeretur, quae ex novis vectigalibus per quinquennium reciperetur. huic toti rationi agrariae senatus adversabatur, suspicans Pompeio novam quamdam potentiam quaeri. Pompeius vero ad voluntatem perferendae legis incubuerat. ego autem magna cum agrariorum gratia confirmabam omnium privatorum possessiones—is enim est noster exercitus hominum, ut tute scis, locupletium—, populo autem et Pompeio—nam id quoque volebam—satis faciebam emptione, qua constituta diligenter et sentinam urbis exhauriri et Italiae solitudinem frequentari posse arbitrabar. sed haec tota res interpellata bello refrixerat. Metellus est consul sane bonus et nos admodum diligit. ille alter ita nihil est, ut plane quid emerit nesciat. 5. haec sunt in re publica, nisi etiam illud ad rem publicam putas pertinere, Herennium quemdam, tribunum plebis, tribulem tuum, sane hominem nequam atque egentem, saepe iam de P. Clodio ad plebem traducendo agere coepisse: huic frequenter interceditur. haec sunt, ut opinor, in re publica. 6. ego autem, ut semel Nonarum illarum Decembrium iunctam invidia ac multorum inimicitiis eximiam quamdam atque immortalem gloriam consecutus sum, non destiti eadem animi magnitudine in re publica versari et illam institutam ac susceptam dignitatem tueri, sed postea quam primum Clodii absolutione levitatem infirmitatemque iudiciorum perspexi, deinde vidi nostros publicanos facile a senatu disiungi, quamquam a me ipso non divellerentur, tum autem beatos homines—hos piscinarios dico, amicos tuos,—non obscure nobis invidere, putavi mihi

maiores quasdam opes et firmiora praesidia esse
quaerenda. 7. itaque primum eum, qui nimium
diu de rebus nostris tacuerat, Pompeium, adduxi in
eam voluntatem, ut in senatu non semel sed saepe
multisque verbis huius mihi salutem imperii atque
orbis terrarum adiudicarit. quod non tam interfuit
mea—neque enim illae res aut ita sunt obscurae,
ut testimonium, aut ita dubiae, ut laudationem
desiderent—quam rei publicae, quod erant quidam
improbi, qui contentionem fore aliquam mihi cum
Pompeio ex rerum illarum dissensione arbitraren-
tur. cum hoc ego me tanta familiaritate coniunxi,
ut uterque nostrum in sua ratione munitior et in re
publica firmior hac coniunctione esse possit. 8.
odia autem illa libidinosae et delicatae iuventutis,
quae erant in me incitata, sic mitigata sunt comi-
tate quadam mea, me unum ut omnes illi colant:
nihil iam denique a me asperum in quemquam fit,
nec tamen quidquam populare ac dissolutum, sed
ita temperata tota ratio est, ut rei publicae constantiam praestem, privatis rebus meis propter
infirmitatem bonorum, iniquitatem malevolorum,
odium in me improborum adhibeam quamdam
cautionem et diligentiam, atque ita tamen his novis
amicitiis implicati sumus, ut crebro mihi vafer ille
Siculus insusurret [Epicharmus] cantilenam illam
suam:

Νᾶφε καὶ μέμνασ' ἀπιστεῖν. ἄρθρα ταῦτα τᾶν φρενῶν.

ac nostrae quidem rationis ac vitae quasi quamdam
formam, ut opinor, vides. 9. de tuo autem negocio saepe ad me scribis, cui mederi nunc non possumus. est enim illud senatus consultum summa

pedariorum voluntate, nullius nostrum auctoritate factum. nam, quod me esse ad scribendum vides, ex ipso senatus consulto intelligere potes aliam rem tum relatam, hoc autem de populis liberis sine causa additum: et ita factum est a P. Servilio filio, qui in postremis sententiam dixit, sed immutari hoc tempore non potest. itaque conventus, qui initio celebrabantur, iam diu fieri desierunt. tu si tuis blanditiis tamen a Sicyoniis numulorum aliquid expresseris, velim me facias certiorem. 10. commentarium consulatus mei Graece compositum misi ad te: in quo si quid erit quod homini Attico minus Graecum eruditumque videatur, non dicam, quod tibi, ut opinor, Panhormi Lucullus de suis historiis dixerat, se, quo facilius illas probaret Romani hominis esse, idcirco barbara quaedam et σόλοικα dispersisse: apud me si quid erit eius modi, me imprudente erit et invito. Latinum si perfecero, ad te mittam. tertium poëma exspectato, ne quod genus a me ipso laudis meae praetermittatur. hic tu cave dicas, τίς πατέρ' αἰνήσει; si est enim apud homines quidquam quod potius sit, laudetur: nos vituperemur, qui non potius alia laudemus. quamquam non ἐγκωμιαστικὰ sunt haec, sed ἱστορικά, quae scribimus. 11. Quintus frater purgat se multum per litteras et adfirmat nihil a se cuiquam de te secus esse dictum. verum haec nobis coram summa cura et diligentia sunt agenda: tu modo nos revise aliquando. Cossinius hic, cui dedi litteras, valde mihi bonus homo et non levis et amans tui visus est et talis, qualem esse eum tuae mihi litterae nunciarant. Idibus Martiis.

XX.

(*Romae. Metello, Afranio coss.* 694.)

Cicero Attico S.

1. Quum e Pompeiano me Romam recepissem a. d. IIII Idus Maias, Cincius noster eam mihi abs te epistolam reddidit, quam tu Idib. Febr. dederas. ei nunc epistolae litteris his respondebo. ac primum tibi perspectum esse iudicium de te meum laetor, deinde te in iis rebus, quae mihi asperius a nobis atque nostris et iniucundius actae videbantur, moderatissimum fuisse vehementissime gaudeo, idque neque amoris mediocris et ingenii summi ac sapientiae iudico. qua de re quum ad me ita suaviter, diligenter, officiose, humaniter scripseris, ut non modo te hortari amplius non debeam, sed ne exspectare quidem abs te aut ab ullo homine tantum facilitatis ac mansuetudinis potuerim, nihil duco esse commodius quam de his rebus nihil iam amplius scribere. quum erimus congressi, tum, si quid res feret, coram inter nos conferemus. 2. quod ad me de re publica scribis, disputas tu quidem et amanter et prudenter et a meis consiliis ratio tua non abhorret—nam neque de statu nobis nostrae dignitatis est recedendum neque sine nostris copiis intra alterius praesidia veniendum et is, de quo scribis, nihil habet amplum, nihil excelsum, nihil non summissum atque populare—, verum tamen fuit ratio mihi fortasse ad tranquillitatem meorum temporum non inutilis, sed me hercule rei publicae multo etiam utilior quam mihi, civium improborum impetus in me reprimi, quum hominis

amplissima fortuna, auctoritate, gratia fluctuantem sententiam confirmassem et a spe malorum ad mearum rerum laudem convertissem. quod si cum aliqua levitate mihi faciendum fuisset, nullam rem tanti aestimassem, sed tamen a me ita sunt acta omnia, non ut ego illi adsentiens levior, sed ut ille me probans gravior videretur. 3. reliqua sic a me aguntur et agentur, ut non committamus ut ea, quae gessimus, fortuito gessisse videamur. meos bonos viros, illos quos significas, et eam, quam mihi dicis obtigisse, Σπάρταν, non modo numquam deseram, sed etiam, si ego ab illa deserar, tamen in mea pristina sententia permanebo. illud tamen velim existimes, me hanc viam optimatum post Catuli mortem nec praesidio ullo nec comitatu tenere. nam, ut ait Rhinton, ut opinor,

Οἱ μὲν παρ' οὐδέν εἰσι, τοῖς δ' οὐδὲν μέλει.

mihi vero ut invideant piscinarii nostri aut scribam ad te alias aut in congressum nostrum reservabo. a curia autem nulla me res divellet, vel quod ita rectum est vel quod rebus meis maxime consentaneum vel quod a senatu quanti fiam minime me poenitet. 4. de Sicyoniis, ut ad te scripsi antea, non multum spei est in senatu. nemo est enim iam qui queratur. qua re, si id exspectas, longum est. alia via, si qua potes, pugna. quum est actum, neque animadversum est ad quos pertineret et raptim in eam sententiam pedarii cucurrerunt. inducendi senatus consulti maturitas nondum est, quod neque sunt qui querantur et multi partim malevolentia, partim opinione aequitatis delectantur. 5. Metellus tuus est egregius consul: unum reprehendo, quod ocium nunciari e Gallia non magno opere gaudet. cupit, credo, triumphare. hoc vellem mediocrius: caetera egregia. Auli filius vero ita se gerit, ut eius consulatus non consulatus sit, sed Magni nostri ὑπώπιον. 6. de meis scriptis misi ad te Graece perfectum consulatum meum. cum librum L. Cossinio dedi. puto te Latinis meis delectari, huic autem Graeco Graecum invidere. alii si scripserint, mittemus ad te, sed, mihi crede, simul atque hoc nostrum legerunt, nescio quo pacto retardantur. 7. nunc, ut ad rem meam redeam, L. Papirius Paetus, vir bonus amatorque noster, mihi libros eos, quos Ser. Claudius reliquit, donavit. quum mihi per legem Cinciam licere capere Cincius amicus tuus diceret, libenter dixi me accepturum, si attulisset. nunc si me amas, si te a me amari scis, enitere per amicos, clientes, hospites, libertos denique ac servos tuos, ut scida ne qua depereat. nam et Graecis his libris, quos suspicor, et Latinis, quos scio illum reliquisse, mihi vehementer opus est. ego autem cotidie magis, quod mihi de forensi labore temporis datur, in his studiis conquiesco. per mihi, per, inquam, gratum feceris, si in hoc tam diligens fueris quam soles in iis rebus, quas me valde velle arbitraris, ipsiusque Paeti tibi negocia commendo, de quibus tibi ille agit maximas gratias, et, ut iam invisas nos, non solum rogo, sed etiam suadeo.

NOTES.

LETTER I.

Epitome of Contents] § 1—3 *A summary of his position as candidate for the consulship, together with a sketch of his probable competitors.* § 3—5 *The reasons of his refusal to act as counsel for Caecilius in his case against A. Caninius Satrius.* § 5 *His acknowledgments for the receipt of a statue.*

§ 1 *Petitionis*]=*prensationis*, as Cicero's *petitio* or formal canvass for the consulship would not begin before the ensuing year. It was usual however to employ the year which immediately followed the praetorship in forming a general interest, and it is to this private canvass that Cicero now alludes. 'The prospects of my canvass in which I know you take the deepest interest are, to make a guess at them, something as follows.'

Unus] 'alone,' for Antonius and Cornificius, though mentioned below as intending candidates, are nowhere said to have begun their canvass. It is therefore quite needless to understand *unus* in the sense of 'especially' on the analogy of the Greek εἷς [Soph. *Trach.* 460, *Oed. rex* 1380] and of such passages as Verg. *Aen.* II. 426 and *Cat.* XXII. 10, if indeed in the latter instance the word is not rather to be explained in its later sense as equivalent to τις.

P. Galba] P. Sulpicius Galba, a patrician, who is mentioned with praise in the *or. pro Mur.* VIII. 17.

Sine fuco ac fallaciis] 'They say him nay in primitive fashion and without ceremony or disguise.' There can be little doubt that this is the right punctuation, in confirmation of which we may instance the similar expression *fucosi suffragatores* (Q. Cic. *de pet. cons.* IX. 35). Manutius on the other hand would take the words *more maiorum* in the sense of 'without bribery,' and refer *sine fuco ac fallaciis* to *prensat* rather than *negatur*.

Praepropera] 'Premature,' both in *time* and *place:* the *comitia tribunicia*, which was the first election in the year, being the recognised time, and the *Campus Martius* the recognised place.

Ita...ut] 'For they generally refuse him their votes on the plea that they are bound to reserve them for me. So I think it must further my interest as the news gains ground that my friends are being found so numerous.'

Cogitaramus] For the epistolary tense cf. Madv. 345.

Proficisci]=*profecturum esse*, as in II. 6. 2 *quando te proficisci istinc putes fac ut sciam*, and again in IV. 16. 12. Boot.

Cincius] L. Cincius, an agent of Atticus, to judge from such passages as VII. 1, VIII. 2, XVI. 17.

a.d. XVI] We may without hesitation reject the old reading *ad* in favour of *a.d.* as the day for the election of tribunes in the Campus Martius would not be left in doubt as the word *ad* would imply.

Qui videantur] "So far as they can be ascertained."

Antonius] C. Antonius Hybrida was Cicero's colleague in the aedileship and praetorship and afterwards in the consulate.

Cornificius] Q. Cornificius 'iudex justissimus' (*or. in Ver.* I. 10. 30). He was Cicero's colleague in the augurship and tribune in the consulship of Metellus and Hortensius.

Ut frontem ferias] To attach these words to the foregoing sentence, as Nobbe edits them, is to destroy utterly the force of the climax. 'I can fancy your smile or rather sigh at this news. To make you tear your hair, Caesonius is thought possible by some.'

In illustration of the phrase *ut frontem ferias*, cf. Dion. Hal. X. 9 παίοντες τὰ μέτωπα, and Cic. *Brut.* LXXX. 278.

Mr Watson regards *ingemuisse* as a sign of grief 'at the impending defeat of a man of good character.' But it seems invidious to draw this distinction when the candidates mentioned in connection with him (e.g. Galba and Caesonius) were little inferior in standing and reputation to Cornificius. Moreover the words *in hoc* must surely refer to the past sentence as a whole. The improbability of Galba's canvass being attended with success, admirable as his character was, may be gathered from Q. Cic. *de pet. cons.* VII. and, as it appears to me, it is the fact of their candidature rather than the likelihood of their rejection which is to excite the mirth and indignation of Atticus. Compare the precisely similar criticism on the candidates of a later year (*Ep.* 17. 1). *Rides? non sunt haec ridicula, mihi crede.*

Caesonium] M. Caesonius, a colleague of Cicero in the aedileship. Cf. *or. in Verr.* I. 10. 29 *homo in rebus iudicandis spectatus et cognitus.*

Aquilium] C. Aquilius (as Orelli writes the name) Gallus, an able lawyer (cf. *Brut.* XLII, *de offic.* III. 14), and the colleague of Cicero in the praetorship.

Denegat et] *denegans,* Boot, a piece of latinity which I should be very reluctant to ascribe to Cicero: while the *denegavit et iuravit* edited by Schütz, Klotz and others is very objectionable on the score of rhythm. Moreover the reading of the text is easily defensible, if we suppose that the change from the present to the aorist tense is intended to mark the difference between the more general fact of his refusal and the definite cause of it: 'at any rate he declares the contrary and has put in a plea of ill-health.' A special explanation of this kind would be required from one who thus stopped short in his career of office

The phrase *iurare morbum* occurs again in *Ep. ad Att.* XII. 13. 2, and may be compared with the similar *excusare morbum.*

In *regnum iudiciale* we may notice a playful allusion to the idea entertained by Aquilius of his own importance in the courts. That the boast was no empty one may be inferred from the *or. pro Caec.* cap. XXVII, where his influence as a *iurisconsultus* is admitted in the strongest possible terms.

Catilina] L. Sergius Catiline, who was at this time excluded from the right of suing for the consulship lying as he did under a charge of extortion in Africa, where he had been praetor A.U.C. 687. Yet, after assuming his guilt in these explicit terms, Cicero in the very next letter is preparing to undertake his defence.

Catiline was acquitted to the disgrace of the judges, and in all probability by the collusion of Clodius who was prosecutor on the occasion. Whether Cicero was his counsel in the case is a matter of doubt. For the whole question and its connection with the date of the subsequent letter, see Mr Forsyth's *Life of Cicero,* p. 87.

Meridie non lucere] 'if the judges can bring themselves to declare that the sun does not shine at noon,' or in other words that 'black is white.'

Auli filio] al. *Aufidio,* by which A. Titus Aufidius would probably be meant who is mentioned in *Brut.* XLVIII. as a jurist, and in the *or. pro Flac.* as praetor in Asia. But the reading of the text is preferred by the best editors, and the allusion is to L. Afranius, a creature of Pompeius, who was consul with Metellus A.U.C. 694. 'A nobody and the son of a nobody' is perhaps the idea.

Palicanus] M. Lollius Palicanus, another candidate of the same stamp, as we may gather from an incident which is related of him in Val. Max. III. 8. 3.

He had been a tribune of the people, and is referred to again in connection with Afranius in I. 18. 5, while in *Brut.* LXXII. he is described as *contionibus turbulentis aptissimus*.

§ 2 *De iis qui nunc petunt*] 'Of those who are standing for the present year Caesar is considered safe. The struggle is thought to lie between Thermus and Silanus: who however are so threadbare in friends and reputation that it seems to me perfectly possible that Curius may be pitted against them. But I am alone in this opinion. It suits my interest best, I think, for Thermus to be returned with Caesar: for, supposing him to stand over for another year, there is no one of the present candidates who is likely to prove a more formidable rival; more particularly as he is conducting the repairs of the Flaminian way, a work now approaching its completion.'

Qui nunc petunt] i.e. for office in 64 B.C. As regards the date of this and the subsequent letter I have followed the ordinary chronology with Klotz, Nobbe and the majority of the editors. On the other hand Schütz and Matthiae would refer both to the previous year.

Caesar] Lucius Iulius Caesar, who was in fact returned with Thermus. For his intervention after the murder of Caesar see in particular *Phil.* VIII. 1. 1, and again XII. 7. 18.

Thermus] Minucius Thermus, adopted into the patrician gens *Marcia*, and mentioned in the Fasti as C. Marcius Figulus. He is supposed to be the Q. Minucius Thermus to whom some of Cicero's letters are addressed, a noted partisan of Pompeius in the civil war. Meriv.

Silano] Decius Iulius Silanus, who was consul with L. Licinius Muraena A. U. C. 691. O.

Ab amicis]=*ex parte amicorum* 'in regard to friends.' The construction is apparently a favourite one with Cicero. Cf. *Ep.* VIII. 14. 1 [tempus] *quod magis debuerit mutum esse a litteris:* III. 17. 1 [litteras] *exploratas a timore*, and *or.*

pro Caec. XXXII. *si planum facit ab se,* where *ab se* is equivalent to *ex sua parte.*

Curium] *Turium,* Boot, and with some probability, as he is mentioned in the Brutus [cap. LXVII] in the following terms: *L. Turius parvo ingenio, sed multo labore, quoquo modo poterat, saepe dicebat. Itaque ei paucae centuriae ad consulatum defuerunt.* But his objection to the received reading on the ground that Curius was a man of infamous character and had in consequence been removed from the senatorial roll [Sall. *bell. Cat.* XVII.] is of little weight, as it is Cicero's intention to disparage Thermus and Silanus by the suggestion of some worthless competitor.

Obducere] ἀντιπαράγειν. This is, according to Boot, the only passage in Cicero where the word is found in this sense.'

Curator viae Flaminiae] Merivale quotes this passage as an illustration of the trifling circumstances which might often determine the choice of a consul. The *via Flaminia* led from the Porta Flumentana through Etruria to Ariminum, and was designed by the censor C. Flaminius A. U. C. 533.

Cum Caesare cons.] *quae cum erit absoluta sane facile eum libenter nunc ceteri consuli acciderim* is the unintelligible reading of the best MS, for which Schütz proposes the following: *Quae tunc erit absoluta sane facile. eo libens Thermum Caesari consulem accedere viderim.* The other emendations which have been suggested are for the most part unsatisfactory. Perhaps the only point which we can determine with any degree of certainty is that the words 'quae tunc erit absoluta' or their equivalent in meaning should form the end of the past sentence rather than the commencement of the new. But, with this exception, the reading adopted by Schütz appears to me to be open to objection on several points: e.g. the position of the words 'sane facile' at the close of a sentence: the introduction of the proper name *Thermus* after so short an interval and when there has been no change of subject: and lastly the unusual character of the concluding phrase 'Caesari consulem accedere viderim,' an objection to which the emendation of Gronovius 'Caesari consulem addiderim' is likewise open.

On the strength of many similar passages we may fairly I think regard the words 'sane facile' as introductory to the new sentence, while the substitution of 'eum' for 'Thermum' is only a return to the reading of the MS. Of the word 'factum' I speak with less confidence. It is however the recognised phrase and, in addition to other passages, occurs in *Ep.* 16. 13 of the present book: 'sed heus tu! videsne consulatum illum nostrum, quem Curio ante ἀποθέωσιν vocabat, si hic *factus* erit, fabulam mimum futurum?'

Informata] *Informare* like *adumbrare* and the Greek ὑποτυπόω and σκιαγραφέω is used of painting or sketching in outline: 'my general impression of the candidates.'

Nos in omni mun. cand.] 'For myself, I shall spare no pains on my canvass: and, as Gaul seems to exercise a considerable influence upon the voting, I may possibly take a trip there in September, as soon as the Roman law-courts have cooled down for the vacation, on a mission to Piso, but so as to be home again in January. As soon as I have got an insight into the intentions of our great men you shall know the result. With this exception, my path is clear: that is in relation to the civilian candidates.'

Gallia] i.e. Gallia Cispadana. For the extent of this influence cf. *Philip.* II. 30, and the treatise *de bell. Gall.* LII. *T. Labienum togatae Galliae praefecit, quo maiore commendatione conciliaretur ad consulatus petitionem.*

Refrixerit] The word is used again in *Ep.* II. 1. 6 of a measure which was indifferently supported; *quod de agraria lege quaeris, sane iam videtur refrixisse.* From the second Verrine oration we find that for the last four months of the Roman year there was an almost entire cessation of business in the Roman law-courts, as the festivals and holidays were crowded into that portion of the year.

Legati] i.e. on a *libera legatio* or honorary embassy to Piso. Caius Calpurnius Piso is meant, who was consul with Acilius Glabrio in the year 67 B.C., and brother of the Marcus Piso in whose consulship Clodius was tried for sacrilege. As governor of Gallia Narbonensis he is the subject of a sarcastic allusion in *Ep.* 13. 2 *praepositumque esse nobis pacificatorem Allobrogum.* At a later period he was accused of peculation, and defended by Cicero (*or. pro Flac.* 39), who procured his acquittal.

Prolixa] Casaubon believes the word to be equivalent to *valde laxa.* But Forcellini suggests with greater probability that the primary idea was that of running water, and that it was originally used of garments. Hence we have *prolixus capillus* of loose-flowing hair. Afterwards it became akin to *propensus.* Thus we have *prolixus animus,* and (*ad div.* VII. 5. 1) *prolixe promittere,* and again (Ter. *And.* V. 8. 20) *age prolixe.* Finally in a speech of Cato (*apud* Aul. Gell. VII. 3) we find *res prolixae* used in the present sense of *secundae.*

Competitoribus urbanis] *civilian* as opposed to *military* rivals. The latter might any day return from a foreign campaign, and prove formidable antagonists. Casaubon would appear to have understood the words in a slightly different sense, to judge from the following note: *quasi dicat, multi nobiles qui absunt.*

Cura ut praestes] i.e. *fac ut mihi caveas ab istis Pompeii asseclis, ne eos competitores habeam,* Schütz. But 'take care to secure me the votes of his retinue' is certainly the more natural interpretation of the words, and more in accordance with the ordinary usage of *praestare.*

Illam manum] i.e. the influential voters who had accompanied Pompeius on his Mithridatic campaign. The phrase *praestare illam manum* may refer to their *votes* or else to their *indirect influence.* It is not necessary to confine it to the latter, as from the sentence which follows it seems clear that some of them, if not Pompeius himself, would be able to attend in person at the election. The explanation suggested by Boot is scarcely satisfactory : *potest tamen quoque indicari opera et auxilium Pompeii. Hac ratione scriptores Graeci utuntur voc.* χείρ.

§ 3 *Pervelim*] 'But there is a matter, by the way, for which I am extremely anxious to secure your forgiveness. Your uncle Caecilius, who has lost a large sum of money by the failure of Varius, has commenced legal proceedings with his brother Satrius for the possession of the property which he accuses him of having received from Varius by a fraudulent bill of sale. The rest of the creditors are making common cause with him, and amongst them Lucullus and Scipio and the person whom they suppose will act as auctioneer if the property should come to the hammer, one Pontius by name. But it is absurd to be discussing the auctioneer at this stage of the proceedings. Caecilius has requested me to appear against Satrius.'

Fratre] Mr Watson notices that in this case, supposing *fratre* to have its usual meaning, one of the two brothers must have changed his name by adoption, or else they must have been brothers on the mother's side.

Dolo malo.] The adjective has been referred by some to *mancipio,* but, besides being the recognised formula in use on such occasions (cf. *de off.* III. 14. 60), the rhythm of the sentence would alone be enough to shew that the words 'dolo malo' cannot possibly be separated. In the present instance the fraud consisted in the illegal transfer of property which ought to have been forthcoming to pay Caecilius and the other creditors.

Lucullus] Lucius Licinius Lucullus is probably meant, the friend of Caecilius as we are told by Nepos in his life of

Atticus, cap. V. As he had by this time returned from his campaign in Asia against Mithridates there is no need to suppose, with Manutius and others, that his brother Marcus is the person referred to.

P. Scipio] He was afterwards adopted by Metellus under the name of Q. Caec. Metellus Pius Scipio. In the civil war he espoused the cause of Pompeius, and killed himself after the battle of Thapsus in B.C. 46.

Magistrum] We have no one word in English to express the various relations of the *magister* in a Roman case of bankruptcy. He was usually selected from the number of the creditors, and was at once auctioneer and assignee of the proceeds of the sale which he was appointed to conduct in their interests. (Cf. *or. pro Quint.* XV. 50.) Trs. 'receiver.'

L. Pontius] L. Pontius Aquila. Cf. *ad Att.* V. 2. 1, and *Philip.* XIII. 13. 27.

Nunc cognoscere] There seems to be no good reason for discrediting the reading of the text: which is at any rate sufficiently intelligible. 'The question as to who is to be receiver is premature and absurd when we do not as yet so much as know whether Satrius will be condemned or his property sold.' On the other hand Madvig's emendation: *verum hoc ridiculum est de magistro. Nunc cognosce rem:* which Klotz and Boot have admitted into their text, ingenious as it undoubtedly is, appears to me to be somewhat devoid of meaning, for, without the addition of the words *nunc cognoscere*, it is quite impossible to see anything ludicrous in the mention of an auctioneer. Boot raises an objection to the reading *cognoscere* on the following ground: 'Vulgo *putabant* Pontium magistrum fore; sed, quam diu incertum erat, utrum bona Varii venirent necne, de magistro *cognoscebat* nemo.' But *cognoscere* is 'to take into consideration,' and the opposition which he discovers between it and *putant* does not appear to me to exist.

Observat] A stronger word than *colere* but used much in the same sense. Cf. *Ep.* 13. 2 *sum enim ab observando homine perverso liber.*

L. Domitium] Lucius Domitius Ahenobarbus was consul with Appius Claudius Pulcher A.U.C. 699, and in his praetorship proved a good friend to Cicero during the time of his banishment.

§ 4 *Demonstravi*] 'I pointed this out to Caecilius, at the same time assuring him that, had the suit been confined to himself and Satrius, I would have done my best to oblige him, but, under present circumstances and in a case which affected the whole body of the creditors, all of them men of distinction, who might easily protect their interests without the aid of a lawyer specially retained by Caecilius on his own account, it was only fair that he should shew some consideration for my feelings and convenience.'

Perhiberet] *praeberet* Corrad. but the word is technical in the sense of παρέχεσθαι, *in iudicium patronum adducere.*

Officio meo] i.e. his obligations to Satrius for his past services: *tempori*, his critical position as a candidate for the consulship.

Homines belli] 'than is usual with your thorough gentleman.' Cf. Quint. *de pet. cons.* XI. *belle negandum est, ut demonstres necessitudinem, ostendas quam moleste feras, aliis te id rebus exsarturum persuadeas.*

Bellus is here equivalent to *humanus.* On the other hand in Catullus and Martial (III. 63) it is used to denote a fop. It is quite possible that a covert allusion may be intended to the manners of Caecilius, which, as we are told elsewhere, were anything but refined or courteous.

Refugit] 'declined the acquaintance which had sprung up between us during the past few days.'

Abs te peto] 'I beg of you to make allowance for me in the matter, and to believe that I was debarred by feelings of common courtesy from taking part against a friend in his hour of need, when his entire reputation was at stake, and when moreover he had just done his best for me in word and deed.'

Summam existimationem] '*Summa existimatio* est res a qua omnis eius existimatio pendet et in discrimen venit : at *summa respublica* est res in qua vertitur salus totius reipublicae.' Graev.

Ambitionem] 'Self-interest' in the matter of his canvass.

ἐπεὶ οὐχ ἱερ.] sub. ἀρνύσθην, 'For indeed the prize is a grand one.' A quotation from *Il.* XXII. 159. Cf. also Verg. *Aen.* XII. 794 *neque enim levia aut ludicra petuntur Praemia.*

Uno] 'mainly.' Cf. *Ep.* 18. 3 *duo firmamenta reipublicae per me unum constituta* and note on § 1 of the present letter.

§ 5 *Hermathena*] For the characteristics of these statues, see note on *Ep.* I. 10. 3. 'I am wonderfully charmed with the statue you have sent me, and it is so happily placed that you would fancy my school to be an offering at its feet. Best love.'

Eius] So Klotz and Boot for ἡλίου, which is retained by Nobbe, though entirely unintelligible. Schütz would read *illius*, but in the similar passage of *Ep.* 4. 3 *eius* is the word used, and as an emendation it is perhaps scarcely more violent.

Gymnasium] i.e. a school for study and recreation, which he had designed in his Tusculan villa on the model of the old gardens of the Academe. The villa itself had once been in the possession of Sulla and was situated about twelve miles from Rome.

LETTER II.

Epitome of Contents] § 1. *The birth of a son. His intention of defending Catiline.* § 2. *A request that Atticus will come to Rome with all possible speed.*

§ 1 *C. Marcio Figulo*] The Thermus mentioned in I. 1. 2. The date of this letter is remarkable as referring in all probability to the day when the new consuls were *elected*, not to that on which they came into office.

That the *consules designati* were often mentioned simply as *consules* is clear from *Ep. ad. Att.* VII. 8, *Phil.* XIV. 3. 8: but in this instance Cicero had probably a special reason for departing from the usual formula, as he may have wished to notify with precision the day on which his son was born. The above explanation, which is countenanced by Schütz, is likewise supported by the contents of the letter, for Catiline was put on his defence in the consulship of Cotta and Torquatus, when Caesar and Figulus were the consuls elect for the ensuing year. The alternative involves the assumption that Catiline was twice tried for different offences.

Filiolo] Marcus. Mr Watson has collected the details of his life, which, though eventful in itself, left little mark on the history of his times.

Catilinam] 'I am preparing to defend my rival Catiline. We have the very judges we wanted, and the prosecutor is quite content. If acquitted, I trust he will work more heartily with me in the matter of my canvass. If otherwise, I shall bear it like a man.' The whole of this incident—whether as regards his readiness to undertake the defence of a man whose guilt (he admits) was as patent as the noonday sun, or the suggestion of underhand play in the *reiectio iudicum*, or the motive which influenced his conduct on the occasion—is in the highest degree discreditable to Cicero. Catiline was favoured in his canvass by Crassus and Caesar, and it was the fear of their influence and the desire for some compromise

which induced Cicero to promise his services. Whether
he actually defended him is still a matter of doubt. The
evidence, such as it is, is slightly in favour of Asconius who
decides the question in the negative. The fact that Cicero
abuses the court which acquitted him (*or. in tog. cand.*) is
not decisive either way: witness his treatment of Fidicu-
lanius Falcula in the *or. pro Caec.* as compared with his
eulogies on the same individual at the Cluentian trial.

Accusatoris] Publius Clodius, who, for a consideration,
is said to have waived his right of challenging the judges.
(*or. de har. resp.* cap. XX.) If so, the expression *summa
accusatoris voluntate* is sufficiently explained. In the *or.
in Pis.* X. 23 a member of the same family (Sex. Clodius) is
charged with a similar offence.

Sin aliter acciderit] i.e. 'if he declines to cooperate with
me,' and not in reference to his possible condemnation—for
in the latter case he would of course be unable to stand for
the consulship.

§ 2 *Tuos familiares*] As for instance, Crassus and C.
Caesar, who were notoriously adverse to Cicero's interests,
and perhaps also Philippus, Hortensius and Lucullus, whom
he refers to again under the name of 'piscinarios nostros'
(*Ep.* 19. 6) as jealous of his influence in the state. The
cause of this feeling is illustrated by the following passage
from Sal. *Cat.* 23: *Pleraque nobilitas invidia aestuabat et
quasi pollui consulatum credebant si eum quamvis egregius
homo novus adeptus foret.* If an additional motive is required it may be found in the devotion shewn by Cicero to
the special interests of Pompeius.

Ianuario ineunte] We have in this another proof that the
consuls Caesar and Figulus were only *elect* at the present time:
for, had they been actually in office, the January of 691 must
have been the one to which Cicero alludes, and by that time
the services of Atticus would have been useless. Besides we
know from other sources that as a matter of fact he was in
Rome before the commencement of that year.

LETTER III.

Epitome of Contents] § 1. *The absence of Atticus and
its fatal consequences.* § 2 *A plea for his return, and an
acknowledgment of the statues received from him.* § 3 *The
inability of the writer to pacify Lucceius. The betrothal of
his daughter to Piso.*

§ 1 *Mortuam esse*] It is quite impossible that this can be
a serious statement, though all the commentators appear to

have regarded it as such. It is no doubt a piece of pleasantry, the object of which was twofold : (1) to hasten the return of Atticus by shewing how much he was missed: (2) to deride the easy going philosophy of his friend Saufeius. 'Regret for your absence has been the death of your grandmother, combined with her fears that the Latin states would not be true to their allegiance, and bring the usual victims to the Alban mount. Saufeius, I imagine, will send you the comfort you require on the occasion.'

Quod verita sit] *deridet suspiciosae aniculae inanem superstitionem.* Man.

Latinae] sub. *civitates*, nor can I conceive why the editors should have suggested either *feriae* (as Boot), with which the expression *in officio manere* is entirely incompatible, or *faeminae* (as Billerbeck), a word which could scarcely have been omitted. Add to which, as Schütz remarks, women had nothing to do with the ceremonial on the occasion. The yearly festival of the *Feriae Latinae* was instituted by Tarquinius Superbus with the express object of retaining his hold over the more distant *civitates* by requiring from them this token of allegiance.

Rei] With the Epicureans death was no evil, and it is in reference to this view that Cicero uses the matter of fact word *rei* in announcing to Atticus his imaginary loss. If we are to regard the communication as a serious one this pleasantry is most ill-timed : but against this view we have the fact that in *Ep.* IV. 6. 1, where he is alluding to an actual loss, Cicero speaks in very different language of Saufeius and his school.

Saufeium] A friend of Atticus and, like himself, a follower of the Epicurean school, of the tenets of which he was an energetic exponent; cf. *Ep.* II. 8. 1 *quamquam licet me Saufeium putes esse, nihil me est inertius.* The spirit of the passage is something to this effect: 'Under the circumstances I may send you my condolences by proxy, and what is more by a correspondent whose philosophy is of a kind to suit your case.'

§ 2 *Ad alios missis?*] 'is it from report alone, or from a letter of yours to some one else?' The elegance of the expression is lost, if we omit the note of interrogation with Boot and others.

Signa] 'The statues which you have procured for me have been landed at Caieta. I hav'n't seen them as yet, for I have had no opportunity of leaving Rome. I have sent a person to pay for their carriage. My best thanks are due to you for the pains you have taken, and for securing them at so reasonable a price.'

Caietam] The celebrated harbour (now Gaeta) in the neighbourhood of which was Cicero's Formian villa. In *Ep.* 4 he refers to the villa itself under the name of Caieta. For a description of his numerous residences see Mr Forsyth's *Cicero*, pp. 61—66.

Exposita] For the use of the word in the sense of 'landed' cf. Verg. *Aen.* X. 288, *de bell. Gall.* IV. 37.

§ 3 *Amico*] L. Lucceius. He was a man of some literary attainments both as poet and historian (cf. *Ep. ad div.* V. 12), and was courted in consequence by Cicero who wished him to sing his praises. In the year 59 B.C. he was an unsuccessful candidate for the consulship. To judge from *Ep.* 14, which was written in the consulship of Messala and Piso, the difference between himself and Atticus (for the origin of which cf. II. 1) must have lasted for the space of seven years.

Quibus de suspicionibus]=*propter quas suspiciones* rather than *cuius de suspicionibus*.

Sallustium] not the historian, cf. *ad div.* XIV. 4. 11, *ad Att.* XI. 17. 1. 'Sallust, though he was on the spot, I have not been able to restore to his old place in his esteem. I mention this to you because he used to find fault with me for neglecting your wishes. He has now found out by experience that our friend is not very amenable, and that I *did* use my best efforts in your behalf.'

Nec tibi defuisse] I am disinclined to alter the received reading, which may be justified by the analogy of the following passages, the latter of which is recognised by Madvig: Pers. V. 172, and Cic. *pro Caec.* XXIV, *nam qui hoc disputant, si id dicunt, non recte aliquid statuere eos qui consulantur, nec hoc debent dicere*, etc. The alteration proposed by Schütz *nec tibi nec sibi* does not read pleasantly, and, had it formed part of the original text, would scarcely have been corrupted. *Nec meum studium tibi defuisse* appears to me a more probable suggestion, as it reads well, and gives a connection to the two sentences the want of which is certainly felt in the received reading. The objection which Boot raises to the text on the ground that it makes *defuisse* dependent on *expertus est* is surely hypercritical, for the construction may be easily explained as a ζεῦγμα.

Tulliolam] His daughter Tullia was at the time of her betrothal only nine, or at the most eleven, years old.

C. Pisoni] His praises are sung by Cicero in the *Brutus* (cap. LXXVIII.) and elsewhere. At a later period he abandoned his quaestorship in Pontus and Bithynia that he might be near at hand to protect his father-in-law.

LETTER IV.

Epitome of Contents] § 1 *Inducements to Atticus to hasten his visit.* § 2 *The trial of Macer.* § 3 *The decoration of his villas, and his wish to purchase the library of Atticus.*

§ 1 'You are for ever raising my hopes of seeing you. Only the other day, when we thought you were on the point of coming, you suddenly put us off till July. Now I really do propose that, as nearly as your convenience will admit, you come at the date you mention. You will be just in time for my brother's election, you will see me after our long parting, and you can settle your difference with Acutilius. Peducaeus has reminded me to mention this: for we think it better that the matter should be finally settled. My help in arranging it has always been at your service.'

Reiecti sumus] Cf. *Ep.* 18. 7 *qua re etiam legationes reiectum iri puto.*

Quinti fratris comitia] who was a candidate for the aedileship, which he held in the consulship of Cotta and Torquatus.

Acutilianam controversiam] Cf. 5. 4, and again 8. 1. The wording of the latter passage sufficiently shews that the matter in question was a debt due from Atticus to Acutilius, and that, in the opinion of Acutilius, the plea advanced by Atticus for deferring payment was an unsatisfactory one.

Peducaeus] The son of Sextus Peducaeus, the praetor of Sicily, to whom Cicero had been quaestor. He was at present in the employ of Atticus as *procurator.* Others, from the date of the letter, have inferred that the father is meant.

§ 2 'I have brought the business of C. Macer to an end, with the marked approbation of the people. I have done him strict justice; nevertheless by his condemnation I have excited so strong a feeling in my favour as far to outstrip any benefit I might have looked for from himself had I acquitted him.' *Meriv.*

C. Macro] Caius Licinius Macer, an historian and orator (Cic. *Brut.* LXVII). He was accused of peculation under Cicero's praetorian auspices (*or. pro Rabir. Post.* IV), who presided over the *quaestio repetundarum* in virtue of his office. Macer was condemned in spite of the influence of Crassus. A sensational story in reference to his trial and condemnation is found in Plutarch (*Cic.* 9), and again in a different form in Val. Max. IX. 12.

Quum aequi fuissemus] The statement of this transaction, which in any form is not particularly creditable to Cicero, is by no means improved by the force which Boot would attach to the subjunctive *fuissemus: cui quum parcere et favere potuissemus*, sive *quum in eius gratiam maiorem aequitatis* (ἐπιεικείας) *quam iuris rationem habere potuissemus.*

Ex populi existimatione] We may compare the following from Plut. *in Cic.* 11 τὰς κρίσεις ἔδοξε καθαρῶς καὶ καλῶς βραβεῦσαι.

§ 3 *Singulare est insigne*] Boot omits *insigne* from his text, but the sentence is incomplete without it. As regards the punctuation and arrangement of the passage there is considerable difficulty. To place the stop after the words *per mihi gratum est* necessitates the introduction of *est* at the commencement of the following sentence—a verb which is already repeated twice in the space of two lines. A more natural remedy is to supply before *Academiae* the word *et* which is much required, and which may easily have been displaced in a sentence redundant with monosyllables.

Eius] is in this case almost equivalent to *talis* 'a school of this class.' Cf. *me eum offendes, Ep.* 10. 6. A statue of Minerva would be specially appropriate, as the idea of the place was borrowed in the first instance from Athens and the Academe, and its primary object was the culture of the intellect.

Caietam] i. e. *Caietanum praedium*, his estate at Formiae: for so far as we know he had no property nearer Caieta than this.

Abundare] to 'overflow' 'be overstocked' with them. It is better I think to supply *signis* rather than *pecunia*: though either explanation is admissible.

Conserva] 'keep your books together, and do not despair of my one day making them my own. This object attained, I surpass Crassus in wealth and can afford to despise the houses and lands of any man.' *Conserva* may mean 'do not sell them,' or else it may have something of the same sense as *confice bibliothecam* in *Ep.* 4. 'make up, complete your library.'

We are told by Corn. Nepos (*vit. Att.* 13) that Atticus kept a large household of slaves, whom he employed to copy MSS for his own library and also for sale.

Crassum] M. Licinius Crassus. Cf. II. 13. 2 *cuius cognomen una cum Crassi Divitis cognomine consenescit.*

Vicos] may be equivalent to *villas* as in Hor. *Epist.* II. 2. 177, but more probably *vici urbani* are meant, while *villae* will be included in the word *prata*, just as in Martial *domus* is used of a 'mansion' or 'house in town' in contrast with a country residence.

LETTER V.

Epitome of Contents] § 1 *The death of his cousin Lucius.* § 2 *The want of harmony in his brother's household.* § 3 *The infrequency of his letters to Atticus.* § 4 *The affair of Acutilius.* § 5 *The pacification of Lucceius.* § 6 *A wardship case.* § 7 *The decoration of his Tusculan villa.* § 8 *His brother Quintus expected. Terentia's health, and conclusion.*

§ 1 *Fructu*] 'What *enjoyment* at home and abroad.' It is better to take *forensis* as referring to his public life in general rather than to his legal duties in particular: although his cousin must have been of great service to him in the latter, if (as Asconius tells us) he travelled through Sicily with him to aid him in collecting materials for the prosecution of Verres.

Lucii] The son of Lucius Tullius Cicero, the brother of the orator's father. In *de fin.* V. I. I Cicero speaks of him as *fratrem, cognatione patruelem, amore germanum*. He died in the year 686, two years before the consulship of Cicero, and this letter which announces the fact is consequently the earliest of the series. This use of *frater* for *patruelis* is not uncommon. Cf. Madv. *Comm.* in *or. pro Cael.* XXIV. 60.

humanitate et moribus] A hendiadys for *humanis moribus*, 'kindly ways.'

Meo sermone] 'My account of you.'

Adfinem] because of the marriage connection between Quintus and Pomponia, the sister of Atticus. Boot notices this as a more general use of the word *adfinis: Proprie enim ex omnibus Tulliis unus Q. Cicero erat Attici adfinis per nuptias sororis.*

§ 2 *De sorore tua*] To judge from the very amusing account of their family relations which is given in *Att.* V. I. 2 the fault must have been chiefly on her side, and we may fairly hold Quintus excused.

Minorem] by about four years.

§ 3 *De litterarum missione*] *intermissione*, Muretus, which however it is quite unnecessary to introduce into the text. In Demos. πρὸς Νικοστρ. 1251 we have the precisely similar expression ἐξ ἐμφανῶν καταστάσεως, 'the *non*-production of available documents,' and compare likewise τὴν πρὸς ἀλλήλους ἐπιτηδευμάτων ὑποψίαν, 'the *absence of* all curiosity about our neighbours' pursuits.' (Thuc. II. 37.)

§ 4] 'As regards your instructions about Acutilius, I

should have executed them forthwith on my arrival at Rome after our parting, but, as it fell out, there was no need of any such hot haste, and—knowing your tact as I did—I preferred that Peducaeus should be your adviser rather than myself. For after I had lent a listening ear to Acutilius for so many days, whose style of conversation you know by experience, it were surely no hardship to *write* you an account of his grievances when I had made none of *listening* to them, which was, I admit, rather a bore.'

Confeceram] The ordinary explanation of this mood is simpler than to refer it, with Boot, to the *purpose*, as for instance in the phrases *nullum senatus consultum facienti* (I. 14. 5), and *traducit* (I. 18. 4).

Nihil] *Mihi*, Boot: who for some unaccountable reason objects to *nihil*. That there was no need for any particular haste in the matter is sufficiently proved by the fact that two years later (I. 4. 1) it was still in progress.

Illius] Unless the interchange of the names is a typographical error Muretus refers this to Peducaeus: *Cicero dicit molestam sibi fuisse loquacitatem et dicacitatem Peducaei, quam tamen molestiam in Pomponii gratiam patienter devoravit*. But Peducaeus was Atticus' own man of business (I. 4. 1), and the intended contrast is not between the men, but between the words *scribere* and *audire*.

Facultatem dandi] 'Opportunity of sending.'

§ 5 *Cuius*] Lucceius.

Recolligi] i.e. *reconciliari*. Cf. I. 10. 2 for the use of *restituere* in the same sense: *primum tibi de nostro amico placando aut etiam restituendo polliceor*.

Teneo quid dicas] 'I understand your meaning.' *Teneo* is the suggestion of Orelli, and its omission is more easily accounted for than that of *scio* or *video*. Some verb of the kind is required by the sense of the passage and by the word *neque* which follows, for it is quite impossible to explain the construction as an ellipse, which is the suggestion of Muretus. If the reading of the MSS is to be retained, I should prefer to translate: 'You say I ought to gather a few hints as to the line you had better take with him.'

Adfectus] 'In a strange state of mind.' He purposely uses an indefinite word, as the special cause of offence was unknown to himself and his friend.

Contendendum] *Concedendum*, Graev., Ern., but *contendere* and *elaborare* are the words used in the corresponding passages of *Epp.* 8 and 10. 'What pressure we are to use should, I think, depend on your own feelings. So if you will inform me on this point you will find that I have avoided being more busy in the matter than yourself, or more remiss than was consistent with your wishes.'

§ 6 *Tadiana re*] 'Tadius, in respect to his case, tells me you have written him word that there is no need for further anxiety on his part, inasmuch as he has acquired a prescriptive right to the inheritance. I am surprised at your ignorance of the fact, that, in the case of a ward, no possession can give a legal claim.' Schütz gives the following explanation of the passage: Tadius, as self-constituted guardian of an heiress who was still under age, had held her property for the two or more years which in ordinary cases (Ulp. *in fragm.* tit. 19, *or. pro Caec.* XIX. 54) gave a prescriptive right to ownership. By the advice of Atticus he pleads this when the legal guardians of the girl claim the property at his hands. But the property of wards was carefully protected against any such claims, and, more than this, they could only be dispossessed of it by a special decree. In the *or. pro Flac.* XXXIV. 84 *tutela legitima* is used absolutely of a ward's property: *nihil potest de tutela legitima sine omnium tutorum auctoritate deminui.*

§ 7 *Epiroticam*] Near Buthrotrum, or Buthrotus, for the name appears in both forms.

§ 8 *Articulorum dolores*] i.e. *arthritidem*, rheumatism.'

Maxime diligit] 'Sends her best love to your sister and mother.'

LETTER VI.

Epitome of Contents] § 1 *The correspondence between them. The purchase of the house of Rabirius by Fonteius.* § 2 *The settlement of the dispute between Quintus and his wife. The departure of Cicero's father. A further order for statues.*

§ 1 *Non committam*] 'I will not risk being charged by you with remissness in writing. Only take care that with such leisure at your disposal you rival me.'

Dimens. et exaed.] 'Laid out and completed in your mind's eye.' C. Rabirius is the person alluded to, who was prosecuted for treason and defended by Cicero in the time of his consulship.

HS CCCIƆƆƆXXX] For a full explanation of the characters, and the system of reckoning, see Madv. *L. Gr.* XI. § 69.

§ 2 *Arpinatibus praediis*] The estate was called *Arcanum.* Cf. V. 1. 2, and *ad Quin. fr.* III. 1. 1.

Discessit] So Madv. for the more usual *decessit*, and he is followed by Boot and others who are unwilling to believe that Cicero announces his father's death in these brief and unfeeling words. They rely chiefly on the evidence of Asconius, who in his preface to the *or. in toga candida* mentions as a fact that Cicero lost his father during the time of his canvass for the consulship, i.e. four years after the date of the present letter. In default of other direct evidence this appears to me to be conclusive, as the authority of the MSS is of little weight in deciding between two words so perpetually interchanged, if indeed the alteration is necessary, as the verb *decedere* is used by Cicero in both senses. As an instance of the special pleading in our author's behalf against which I have protested in my preface let me quote Billerbeck's comment on the reading *decessit*: 'The shortness of the notice shews how deeply Cicero felt his loss.'

Quae loci sint] 'Suited to the place you know so well.' Cf. *ad div.* VII. 23. 2, where he describes the kind of statue he requires, and objects to a Mars and Bacchante as unsuited to the character of the place.

LETTER VII.

Epitome of Contents] *This letter relates chiefly to the adornment of his Tusculan villa.*

Apud matrem] 'At your mother's house.'

XXCD] The same payment as that which is notified in different characters in § 2 of the following letter. The latter is apparently the correct form, as Madvig, Grant, and the other authorities on the subject would in all cases represent the number 400 by the characters CCCC rather than by those which appear in the text.

LETTER VIII.

Epitome of Contents] § 1 *The health of the mother of Atticus. Allusions to Acutilius, Tadius and Lucceius.* § 2 *His payment to Cincius, and further orders in reference to the statues.* § 3 *The eagerness of Tullia to receive her promised present.*

§ 1 *Negat*] 'He says he has received no advice of any kind from his agent, and can scarcely believe that the difference between you arose from his refusal to give you a guarantee against further claims.' See note on I. 4. 1.

Decidisse] is to settle a difference privately without bringing it before a court. Cf. Cic. *pro Rosc. Amer.* XXXIX. *si* hanc ei rem privatim Sex. Roscius mandavisset, ut cum Chrysogono transigeret atque decideret: and *pro Rosc. Com.* XI. 32 *lite contestata, iudicio damni iniuria constituto, tu sine me cum Flavio decidisti.*

Gratum...iucundum] 'A matter of thanks...a matter of pleasure,' a distinction which is illustrated by the following passages: *Ep.* I. 17. 6 *fuit mihi saepe et laudis nostrae gratulatio tua iucunda et timoris consolatio grata:* III. 24. 2 *nam ista veritas, etiamsi iucunda non est, mihi tamen grata est,* and again *ad div.* IV. 6. 1 *cuius officia iucundiora scilicet saepe mihi fuerunt, nunquam tamen gratiora.*

Mihi amicissimus] In *Ep. ad div.* V. 15. 2 he speaks of his friendship with Lucceius in the strongest possible terms: *tecum vivere possem equidem et maxime vellem: vetustas, amor, consuetudo, studia paria: quod vinclum, quaeso, deest nostrae coniunctioni?*

§ 2 *Pentelici*] 'From the quarries of Pentelicus.' A further explanation of the name is given by Suidas, who refers it to the five lines with which the marble was striped.

Iam nunc] 'Even by anticipation please me mightily.' Cf. Prop. V. 11. 93 'Discite venturam *iam nunc* sentire senectam.' The prospective sense which distinguishes *iam nunc* from the corresponding phrase *nunc iam* is probably to be explained by the fact that in both cases the word *iam* has lost its temporal force.

Caetera] Among which would be included such things as the *typos* and the *putealia sigillata* for which he gives an order in the following letter.

Elegantiae] 'Refined taste.' In the 2nd Book of the *Tusc. disp.* we have a full account of the Academia at Cicero's Tusculan villa, where he tells us that it was laid out with shady walks (*xysti*) and quiet seats (*exedrae*). Like the Greek gymnasium it had two quadrangles, of which the outer corresponded to the ἔξω δρόμος or ξυστός, while the inner one was furnished with seats for philosophical discussion. The Lyceum, to which he refers in *de div.* I. 5 as *superiori gymnasio*, was apparently quite distinct from the Academia in question.

Studio efferimur] 'I am so enthusiastic on the subject.'

Munusculum] 'Is importunate for your present, and duns me as your representative. To speak for myself, I am determined to repudiate rather than to pay.' The *munusculum* in question was no doubt promised on the occasion of her betrothal to Piso. For *appellare* in this sense cf. Cic. *Phil.* II. 29 *appellatus es de pecunia quam pro domo, pro hortis, pro sectione debebas;* and for *abiurare* cf. Plaut. *Curc.* IV.

2. 10 *qui abiurant si quid creditum est.* Boot suggests that the word *dependere* is technical for this particular class of payments, and notices the fact that the legal process available for the guarantor in case of loss was known as *actio depensi* (Gai. III. 127). The word is only used once by Cicero of a monetary payment, and the instance in question supports the above view. Cf. *ad div.* I. 9. 9 *nisi cum Marco diligenter egeris, dependendum tibi est quod mihi pro illo spopondisti.*

LETTER IX.

Epitome of Contents] § 1 *On the subject of their correspondence.* § 2 *His eagerness for the promised statues, and a request for information respecting the Eleusinian mysteries.*

§ 1 *Devenire*] The preposition as in *devius, deverticulum,* &c. denotes the uncertainty of the destination. Cf. *Brut.* XLII. *consideranti, ad quos ista non translata sint, sed nescio quo pacto devenerint.*

§ 2 *Signa Megarica*] i.e. of Megarian marble of the class known as κογχίτης λίθος from the quarries near Amphialus. It was pure white, easy to cut, and full of sea shells. Cf. the following passage from Paus. I. 44, μόνοις δὲ Ἑλλήνων Μεγαρεῦσιν ὁ κογχίτης λίθος ἐστι, καὶ σφίσι καὶ ἐν τῇ πόλει πεποίηται πολλὰ ἐξ αὐτοῦ. ἔστι δὲ ἄγαν λευκὸς καὶ ἄλλου λίθου μαλακώτερος, κόγχαι δὲ αἱ θαλάσσιαι διὰ παντὸς ἔνεισιν.

Arcae nostrae confidito] 'Rely upon my solvency,' 'Trust to the length of my purse.' Cf. *arcae nostrae fiducia* (*ad Quint. fr.* II. 12. 5), and Iuv. *Sat.* III. 143 *quantum quisque sua numorum servat in arca, Tantum habet et fidei.* The allusion is not necessarily to a payment in *ready money,* as some editors would explain it on the analogy of the more technical phrase *ex arca solvere.*

Genus hoc est] 'This is the line my fancy takes. That kind of statuary which is most suitable for a training ground is what I require. Lentulus offers me the use of his ships. Pray attend carefully to my wishes in the matter. Chilius sends you a request, and I second it, for any information you can give us about the rites of the Eumolpidae.'

Lentulus] Schütz regards him as identical with the Lentulus mentioned in I. 19. 2 on the ground that all the other members of the family had held office and were little likely to be engaged in trade. But the latter assumption is somewhat bold, while the contemptuous allusion in *Ep.* 19 suggests an enemy rather than a friend.

Chilius] A poet, and in all probability the guest of Cicero at the present time. He is mentioned on two other occasions in the letters to Atticus, viz. in *Ep.* 12. 2, and again in *Ep.* 16. 15, from the latter of which it may be inferred that he was at one time engaged on a poem in praise of Cicero's consulship.

Εὐμολπιδῶν πάτρια] Gronovius would take Εὐμολπιδῶν in a general sense as equivalent to Ἀθηναίων, but the allusion is in all probability to a proposed poem on the Eleusinian rites, for which Chilius wants a groundwork of facts. An account of the external ceremonial is no doubt all that he requires: for Atticus would probably know as little as himself of the more secret mysteries which it was death to reveal.

LETTER X.

Epitome of Contents] § 1 *An excuse for the brevity of the present letter.* § 2 *The quarrel of Lucceius.* § 3 *The further decoration of his Tusculan villa.* § 4 *His eagerness to secure the library of Atticus.* § 5 *The state of his brother's household.* § 6 *The absence of Atticus from Rome, and his promised present to Tullia.*

§ 1 *Ceramico*] There were two places of this name at Athens, one outside the city, the other within the walls. The allusion in the present case is to the former and more famous of the two, which Thucydides in the funeral oration calls 'the fairest suburb of the city.' It is probable that this villa of Atticus is the one alluded to in the *Leges* (I. 13).

Verum tamen] Resumptive after a parenthesis like the Greek δ' οὖν. Cf. *Ep.* 20. 2. *Sed* and *igitur* are frequently used in the same way, and very rarely *tamen*, of which however Boot quotes two instances, *Brut.* XXVI. 101, and *ad div.* IX. 16. 2.

§ 2 *Amico*] Lucceius, as before. For this use of *restituere* cf. *ad Att.* XV. 4. 1 *decimo kalend. hora* VIII *fere a Q. Fufio venit tabellarius, nescio quid ab eo litterularum, uti me sibi restituerem.*

Subesse] ὑποκεῖσθαι. 'As I cannot discover any strong ground for it.'

§ 3 *Imponas*] 'I should like you to see my statues on board at your own convenience, and anything else you can find that is in character with the place you know so well.'

These *Hermeraclae* and other statues of the same class were either simply *bifrontes* or else composite figures representing the attributes of the two divinities combined in one person. As an illustration of the latter class we have the celebrated description of Vertumnus in Propertius [V. 2].

Scribebam] 'For I am sitting there to write this letter, so that the place itself puts in a word. In addition I give you an order for bas-reliefs for insertion in the plaster walls of my ante-chamber, together with figured curbstones for my two wells.'

Typos] Small figures, usually formed of *terra cotta:* cf. Plin. *H. N.* XXXV. 151 *impressa argilla typum fecit, et cum caeteris fictilibus induratum igni proposuit.*

Atrioli] To distinguish it from the *atrium maius.* Cf. Bek. *Gal.* II. 176 and *Ep. ad Quint. frat.* III. 1. 1 *neque enim satis loci esse videbatur atriolo : neque fere solet nisi in his aedificiis fieri in quibus est atrium maius.*

Putealia] Gk. περιστόμια. In *Verr.* II. 4. 14 the word *sigillati* is used of raised work in silver.

§ 4] 'Take care not to promise your library to any one, whatever ardent admirers it may find. I am hoarding up all my little gleanings in the hope of purchasing it for the comfort of my old age.'

§ 6 *Comitiis meis*] Muretus would explain this in reference to the consular election: while Manutius, Schütz and Abeken understand it of the praetorship. The latter is in all probability the correct view, as we know from other sources (e.g. Plut. *Cic.* IX., *pro leg. Man.* I. 2) that the elections for the *praetor urbanus* were on the occasion of Cicero's canvass twice postponed—a fact which is clearly alluded to in § 2 of the ensuing letter. 'As regards my election I do not forget that I have given you leave of absence, and indeed have never ceased to proclaim it aloud to our mutual friends who are on the look-out for you, that, so far from pressing you to come, I have even put my veto upon it: understanding as I do that you will gain more by attention to your business at home than I should by your presence at my election. And therefore I hope you will be under the impression that I have sent you to your present quarters for the furtherance of my interests. For myself, you will find me both in word and deed as grateful to you as though my successes, whatever they may be, had been gained, not only in your presence, but by your exertions. Little Tullia is for binding you to a day: she gives your representative no peace.'

Permisisse] I can find no other example of this construction. Mr Swinburne however in his *Atalanta in Calydon* (p. 83) makes a somewhat similar use of the verb 'allow :' 'But the gods *Allowed* us, and our days were clear of these.'

Quod intelligam] *Quod intelligo* Boot, making with *agendum esset,* which he has introduced into his text for *agendum est*, an almost hopeless confusion of tenses. On the other hand, the ordinary reading *quod intelligam* is at once the more usual formula, and interferes in no way with the retention of *est*, for which the *esset* of some MSS is an evident corruption.

In the earlier part of the sentence the word *hoc* refers primarily to *permisisse*, and is afterwards by a common construction further explained in the sentence *te non modo non arcessi a me, sed prohiberi*.

Offendes] Cf. § 3 of the next letter: (res) *quas tu incredibile est, quam brevi tempore quanto deteriores offensurus sis, quam reliquisti*.

Diem dat] 'Is for taking the law on you,' as in case the debtor failed to discharge the debt on the appointed day legal proceedings followed as the necessary consequence.

Sponsorem appellat] The editors are almost equally divided on the question of retaining or omitting the negative in the present passage. I have decided to omit it with Schütz, Casaub., Ern. and others, on the ground that no reason can be given for Tullia's change of purpose if (as we can hardly question) *appellat* is to be explained here in the same way as in the parallel passage of *Ep*. 8.

The reading *sponsorem me appellat*, which finds favour with Klotz and Boot, has little to recommend it. The pronoun is certainly not required, and its introduction spoils the terseness of the sentence.

LETTER XI.

Epitome of Contents] § 1 *His negotiations with Lucceius.* § 2 *His canvass for the praetorship.* § 3 *The decoration of his Tusculan villa.*

§ 1] 'I was already taking steps of my own accord, and, on receipt of your two letters written persistently in the same strain, have been thoroughly roused to action. Add to which, Sallust is always at my elbow pressing me to do my best in the matter of Lucceius.'

Adsiduus] In its literal sense. Cf. Hor. *Sat*. I. 1. 82, and the *or. pro Caec*. XXII. where it is used of the labourers who are regularly employed on a farm: *non si coactis hominibus quam si voluntariis aut etiam adsiduis ac domesticis.*

Sallustius] See note on *Ep*. 3. 3.

Immutatae voluntatis] 'This change of feeling.' In Ter. *Andr*. I. 5. 7 we find the word as an adjective in the sense of 'unchanged,' while in the *de Or*. II. 67 *immutata oratio* is used of allegory.

Illud tuum arbitrium] 'That decision of yours in his case,' a more natural expression, as it appears to me, than *illud suum arbitrium*, which Klotz and Boot have admitted into their text, and which could only mean 'the arbitration which is for ever on his lips.'

Nostra adlegatio] 'Diplomacy of mine.' The difference between *legare* and *adlegare* is scarcely so definite as Boot and others have imagined, who would restrict the former word to affairs of state, the latter to those of individuals: a distinction which is not universally observed, as we may gather from the use of the word in Plin. *Pan.* 70 *hoc senatui adlegandum putavi.* More probably the primary idea contained in *adlegatio* is that of *secret* and even *underhand* dealing (cf. Ter. *Andr.* V. 3. 28 *ne credas a me adlegatum*, i.e. *subornatum*), a supposition which accounts for the ordinary use of the word in connection with the private affairs of individuals, and also serves to explain its meaning in the passage quoted above from the *Panegyricus*.

Tanti putaris] 'If only you think it worth the trouble.' I have followed the punctuation of Boot, which, from the position of the word *id* and the rhythm of the sentence, seems to me far preferable to that which is adopted by Klotz and the other editors: *si modo tanti putaris id, quod, si me audies et si humanitati tuae constare voles, certe putabis*.

In nostra potestate fore] Cf. § 2 of the last letter.

Idem] 'I now *on the other hand* seem to distrust my powers.' For this use of *idem* cf. amongst many other passages *de nat. Deor.* I. 43 [Epicurus] *quum optimam et praestantissimam naturam Dei dicat esse, negat idem esse in Deo gratiam*.

Obfirmatior] 'More persistent in this fit of spleen.'

In utro culpa erit] 'Shall still annoy the one who is to blame.' Great exception has naturally been taken to this careless and selfish decision on the part of Cicero. To those whose business it is to explain away the force of all such passages, the following suggestion will probably recommend itself: *scripsit hoc, opinor, Cicero ut Epicureum Attici torporem excitaret. Nihil in tribus est epistolis unde colligas falso queri Lucceium: sunt autem multa quae significent profectam esse ab Attico gravem iniuriam.* Oliv.

§ 2 *Arbitrari*] The omission of the subject *te* is worthy of notice, more especially as C. T. Zumpt (*Verr.* V. 106) quotes this as an instance in which *arbitrari* is used by Cicero as a passive. It may however have been due to the fact that he is quoting from a letter of Atticus. We have a similar instance in *ad div.* II. 13. 5 *haec eo pluribus scripsi, quod nonnihil significabant tuae litterae subdubitare, qua essem erga illum voluntate.*

Designatum] Cf. § 6 of the previous letter, and Merivale's *Life of Cicero* (p. 30): 'He thus complains, in the year when he was preparing to solicit for the praetorship: *No people in Rome are more worried in these days than the candidates; every kind of injustice is permitted towards them.*'

Philadelpho] The *tabellarius*, in all probability one of the slaves of Atticus.

§ 3 *Mire quam*] θαυμαστῶς ὡς.

Quam brevi temp. quam det.] Matthiae instances the following examples of this construction: *or.* I. 3 *in qua difficile est enumerare quot viri quanta scientia fuerint;* and again *or. pro Mil.* XIV. 38 *quem si interficere voluisset, quanta, quoties occasiones quam praeclarae fuerunt.*

LETTER XII.

Epitome of Contents] § 1 *His pecuniary embarrassments, and schemes for raising a loan. The prosecution of Antonius for malversation in his province.* § 2 *The reports spread by one Hilarus.* § 3 *His friendship with Pompeius. The divorce of Mucia. The Clodian scandal.* § 4 *The death of his slave Sositheus.*

§ 1] 'Our Trojan lady is in truth a slow business: and Cornelius has never paid Terentia a second visit. So we must have recourse, I suppose, to Considius and his tribe. For from Caecilius even his relatives cannot extract a penny at anything less than 12 per cent. But, to return to the original question, I never knew anything so shameless, so cunning, so dilatory as our friend: *I am on the point of sending my freedman: Titus has received my instructions:* all mere pretexts for delay. Notwithstanding I have an idea that fortune will befriend us. For his couriers bring me word that Pompeius will press openly for the recall of Antonius, who thereupon will be arraigned before the people.'

Τεῦκρις] The data we possess for the solution of this mystery are briefly as follows :

(1) The mention of the well-known money-lenders, Considius, Axius, Selicius and Caecilius, which marks the question as one of pecuniary accommodation, and points to the embarrassments in which Cicero had involved himself by the purchase of his house on the Palatine in the year after his consulship. In a letter to Sextius, the quaestor of An-

tonius, he states the purchase money at three millions and a half of sesterces, and admits that he had been obliged to borrow largely in order to find the required sum—from Sulla amongst others, whose defence he had undertaken according to Gellius (*N. A.* XII. 12). From this we may infer that Τεῦκρις was some effeminate Roman nobleman from whom he was expecting help of a similar kind. For the disparaging title. cf. Pers. *Sat.* I. 4.

(2) The reference to Cornelius, who may possibly be the agent of Caesar alluded to in *Ep. ad Att.* II. 3. 3 *nam fuit apud me Cornelius, hunc dico Balbum Caesaris familiarem.* It is, however, probable that another Cornelius is meant, of whom mention is made in *Ep. ad div.* V. 6. I. If so, the introduction of his name may throw some light on the remainder of the passage, as he was connected by marriage with Publius Sextius, the quaestor of Antonius, and managed his business at home during his absence in the province.

(3) A far more important hint is given us in the immediate transition to Antonius and his affairs, which follows in the words *sed nescio an* ταὐτόματον ἡμῶν, *nam mihi* &c. This connects the monetary question so closely with the recall and prosecution of Antonius that we can scarcely avoid the inference that the allusion is either to Antonius himself, or to one of his most intimate friends.

At first sight the arguments against the hypothesis that Τεῦκρις and Antonius are identical are clear and telling, and they have been ably marshalled by Schütz. For instance, why should Cicero use the mysterious designation in one sentence, and in the next mention Antonius by name? And why, if he expects money for undertaking his defence, does he in the same breath announce his determination to abandon it? But in spite of these arguments, and even on the strength of them, I believe that Antonius himself is the Τεῦκρις of the text, more especially as an evident motive for concealing his real name in connection with the proposed loan, and also for renouncing all interest in his defence, is supplied by Cicero himself in this very letter. With the story of Hilarus full in view it would scarcely have been well to let the world about him know that he was at that very moment expecting large sums from Antonius, and for the same reason it was only a politic measure to denounce his actions, at least till the scandal of Hilarus had died out: for as a matter of fact he *did* defend him in spite of his present assertions to the contrary. Cf. *or. pro dom.* XVI. Amongst other attempts to veil the nature of the present transaction we may instance the introduction of Terentia's name in place of his own, and also his use throughout of the indefinite plural.

Lentum sane negocium] However, in *Ep.* 12. 7 we find the following: Τεῦκρις *promissa patravit.* Considius is mentioned as a money-lender in Val. Max. IV. 8, Axius in *Ep. ad Att.* X. 11. 2, and Selicius in IV. 18. 3.

Caecilio] The uncle of Atticus. Cf. I. 2. The present passage is quoted in full by Seneca (*Ep.* 118) in illustration of the character of Caecilius. For a further account of his pride and avarice cf. Nep. *Att. vit.* V.

Minore centesimis] In proof that 1 per cent. per month was a heavy rate of interest Boot refers to *ad div.* V. 6. 2, where ½ per cent. (*semissibus*) is mentioned as the current rate at the time. It is noticeable that in the corresponding passage of Seneca's letters the unusual construction *minore centesimis* is replaced by the more ordinary phrase *minoris centesimis*, which was in all probability rejected by Cicero as offensive to the ear.

ταὐτόματον ἡμῶν] κάλλιον βουλεύεται, 'chance is wiser than we,' a line from Menander (Γνωμ. μονοστ. in *fragm. Com. Gr.* IV. p. 361, Meineke). Unless we accept the identity of Τεῦκρις with Antonius, the connection between this passage and the foregoing—Cicero's impecuniosity and Antony's recall—appears to me an insoluble problem.

Aget praetor ad populum] He alludes to the formal motion for the recall and prosecution of Antonius.

Hominem defendere] Yet he had already done so (cf. *Ep. ad div.* V. 6. 4), and afterwards, when Antonius underwent a second and more severe prosecution under the consuls Caesar and Bibulus, he again defended him but without success. (Merivale's *Life and Letters*, p. 59.)

Hoc] 'The following circumstance.' For *accidit* Schütz reads *accedit*. But we should have expected in that case the familiar phrase *accedit quod* without the introductory word *etenim:* for, whenever a verb has come to form part of a phrase, Cicero rarely introduces a word to break the legitimate combination.

§ 2] 'For an event has occurred into the origin and character of which I wish you to look carefully. I have a freedman, one Hilarus by name, a rascally fellow enough, an accountant and client of yours. In connection with him the interpreter Valerius mentions the following report, and Chilius writes me word that it has reached him: that the fellow is closeted with Antonius, who gives out, when he makes his requisitions, that a portion of them is to go to me, and that I have sent out this freedman to look after my share of the gains. I have been seriously annoyed by the report, although not quite believing it. However, the scandal it has raised is considerable.'

Libertum habeo...clientem tuum] From this and similar passages (*or. pro Rosc. Am.* VII. 19, Suet. *Caes.* 2) we find that a *libertinus* could have two *patroni*, one in his character of *libertus*, and the other in that of *cliens*.

Ratiocinatorem] He was probably in the service of Antonius at the present time: or else the word may refer to the post he had originally held in Cicero's establishment.

Valerius] He is mentioned again in *Ep. ad div.* XIV. 2. 2. His duties were to interpret for the ambassadors of subject states on their arrival in Rome.

Partem mihi quaeri] This is usually referred to some secret agreement between them in accordance with which Cicero declined the province in his favour. But such an explanation is quite inconsistent with what we know of the character of Cicero, who, whatever his faults may have been, was certainly not grasping or covetous. Abeken's conjecture, which is endorsed by Merivale, is far more probable: that Antonius had promised him a pecuniary remuneration if he would undertake his defence in the Senate against the prosecution with which he was threatened.

Plancium] The subject of the *or. pro Plancio*, and a staunch friend of Cicero in all his troubles. He was military tribune in Macedonia at the present time.

§ 3 *Amicissimum*] The first mention in these letters of the celebrated friendship between Cicero and Pompeius which (to judge from the account of their relations in *Ep. ad div.* V. 7) must have been somewhat sudden in its growth. Atticus never approved of it: most probably because he had a keener forecaste than Cicero in politics, and believed him to be altogether mistaken in his choice of a patron. In addition to which he may have seen how insincere was the friendship, at any rate on the side of Pompeius.

Muciae] She was the sister of Metellus, and the wife of Pompeius, who, on his return from Asia, divorced her on a suspicion of adultery with C. Caesar.

P. Clodium] For a full account of the matter, cf. Merivale, p. 63.

Quum pro populo fieret] This use of *facere* and *fieri* in the sense of 'sacrificing' (like the Greek ἔρδειν and ῥέζειν) is too well known to require comment. The rites alluded to are those of the *Bona Dea*, celebrated by women alone in the house of the Pontifex Maximus.

Servatum et eductum] A hendiadys: 'was got safely out of the house.'

Servulae] *Serviliae*, al. But the words *ancillarum beneficio* in the speech *de harusp. resp.* XXI, and the corresponding passage in Plutarch's *Life of Cicero* (27), are a sufficient confirmation of the reading in the text.

§ 4] 'What further to tell you I know not; indeed I am too much out of heart to write: for I have lost my reader Sositheus, a pleasant lad, and his death has distressed me more than a slave's death should.'

I cannot be so enthusiastic as Mr Forsyth in praise of the feeling shewn by Cicero on this occasion. To my mind it is greatly spoilt by the allusion to his own condescension, and I prefer in consequence the epigram of Martial on the death of Erotion (V. 37).

ἀναγνώστης] *Latine* 'lector.' Cf. Plin. *Ep.* III. 5.

Quod in buccam venerit] 'Whatever comes uppermost.' Cf. *ad Att.* VII. 10, XII. 1. 2, and Mart. XII. 24. 5.

LETTER XIII.

Epitome of Contents] § 1 *On the subject of their correspondence.* § 2 *His position in the Senate, and an account of the consuls.* § 3 *The Clodian scandal.* § 4 *His relations with Pompeius.* § 5 *His literary works.* § 6 *Messala's purchase of a house, and the affair of* Τεῦκρις.

§ 1] Atticus, after a stay of nearly two years in Rome, a period which included the consulship of Cicero, had now left for Greece, and was writing from the different places at which he halted on the journey.

Iam] 'This makes the third letter which I have received from you.'

Tribus Tabernis] The well-known tavern on the Appian Way between Aricia and the *Forum Appii*.

Ancoris sublatis] I have admitted this alteration with Schütz and the majority of the editors, though feeling strongly that the reading of the MSS, *ancora soluta*, ought not to be so lightly rejected. That *ancoram solvere* can mean to 'weigh anchor,' or that Atticus used it by mistake and

Cicero in *ut scribis* calls attention to the error, is equally impossible. But two other alternatives are to be considered, of which the first and more probable is that *ancoram solvere* is to be taken in the more poetical sense of *navem solvere*, or *funem praecidere*, i.e., to cut the cable which held them to their moorings. The other possible explanation is to suppose that he had already been travelling by sea and that he writes as soon as the ship had *anchored* in port. This is perfectly tenable, as the place from which he writes is not stated, and may, for all we know, have been one of his stopping places on the voyage. Of the other emendations which have been proposed, the following is perhaps the best, *ora soluta*, a phrase which may be illustrated from *Quint.* IV. 2. 1 *conscendi, sublatae sunt ancorae, solvimus oram, profecti sumus.*

Rhetorum] 'Masterpieces,' 'true works of art.' I can see no objection to the phrase 'worthy of a rhetorician.' It is at any rate better than the majority of the readings which are proposed in its place; e.g. *quae fuerunt omnes. Rhetorum more loquuntur.* Orelli's emendation, *quae fuerunt omnes, ut rhetorum pueri loquuntur,* κ.τ.λ., is admitted by Mr Watson, and has certainly much to recommend it.

Humanitatis sparsae sale] 'Garnished with a refined wit.' *Lacessitus*, 'challenged.'

Pellectione relevarit] 'For how few are there who can carry a letter of any weight without first easing the burden by reading it through!'

Quod mihi non...est] The word *notum*, or one equivalent in meaning, is essential to the construction. Orelli proposes *perinde*, which is accepted by Matthiae. 'Moreover it is not all the same to me who goes to Epirus,' i.e. whether he is a trustworthy man or the reverse. Boot is scarcely to be congratulated on his proposed emendation: *quod mihi non bonus est, ut quisque in Epirum proficiscatur.*

Caesis...victimis] As would be done by a general prior to the commencement of a campaign. 'My private opinion is that you have by this time offered sacrifice at the shrine of your Amalthea, and started at once to commence operations on Sicyon.'

Apud Amaltheam] This may be either the nymph herself or the villa in Epirus which she is supposed to have under her care; but *caesis victimis* points to the former interpretation, while the neuter *Amaltheum* is the more usual form in the latter sense. The title denotes the abundant fertility of the place, and we have a similar word in *cornucopia*, which is itself derived from the story of Amalthea.

Orelli however understands it as referring to an old chapel which Atticus had found on the estate, while Mr Watson suggests the following explanation of the name: 'A villa in Epirus so called apparently from containing a room decorated with pictures from the story of Amalthea.' But the word τοποθεσίᾳ in *Ep.* 16. 18 is I think in favour of my view.

Ad Sicyonem oppugnandum] Cf. *Ep.* 19. 9, and 20. 4. It is a playful allusion to certain payments which were due to Atticus from Sicyon, either in his capacity of *publicanus*, or else on account of a loan which he had advanced to the state. The former is the more probable theory, for we find that about this time Sicyon, as one of the *liberi populi*, received certain exemptions from tribute which were an evident loss to the company who farmed her taxes.

A similar conflict between public and private interests is alluded to in connection with the *portorium circumvectionis* (*Ep.* II. 16. 4).

Antonium] *Ep. ad div.* V. 5 is a letter of recommendation from Cicero to Antonius in reference to this visit of Atticus, the special object of which appears to have been the recovery of certain sums which were owing to him in Macedonia.

§ 2] 'Now since your departure events have happened of importance enough to warrant a letter, which must not however be exposed to the risk of being lost, or opened, or intercepted. To begin with then let me tell you that the consul did not ask my opinion first in the Senate, but gave precedence to our peacemaker from Gaul, at which a murmur of disapproval ran through the house. For myself I am pleased rather than otherwise, for I am free from any obligation to a wayward fellow, and at liberty to assert my position in the state in spite of him; while the second speaker in a debate has little less influence than the first, and an independence unfettered by any compliment from the consul.'

Pacificatorem Allobrogum] C. Calpurnius Piso, the brother of the present consul, and himself consul in the year 67 B.C. In his proconsulship he had quelled some slight tumult in Gaul (cf. *or. in Cat.* III. 9. 22). Casaubon infers from the notice in the text that the compliment in question had been paid to Cicero the year before by the consul Silanus.

Admurmurante] For the use of this verb in a *hostile* sense we may compare *or. Verr.* II. 5. 16 *quam valde universi admurmuraverint, quam palam principes contra dixerint*: and again in *Ep.* 16. 4 we have the similar compound *acclamatio* used in a like sense.

Neque me invito] For this use of *neque* cf. *Ep.* 17. 1 *ferre moleste neque aperte dicere.*

Catulus] Q. Lutatius Catulus, who, as Plutarch tells us, was pronounced by the dictator Sulla to be the best man in the state. From all that we know of his character he well deserved the praise. In his note on the present passage Mr Watson gives the following as the order in which the opinions of the house were usually taken: (1) that of the consuls elect, if the debate was held late in the year; (2) of the *princeps senatus;* (3) of some other consular at the discretion of the presiding magistrate.

Consul] Marcus Piso. For another and very different estimate of his character cf. Cic. *or. pro Planc.* V. 12.

Cavillator] 'A scoffer of that peevish school.' For a fuller description of his oratory cf. *Brut.* LXVII. 236. It has been proposed to substitute for *moroso* the extremely doubtful word *mocoso* (μῶκος), but in the passage referred to above *morosus* is the word actually used to denote the peculiarities of his style.

Facie magis quam facetiis] 'Laughable rather from his expression than his expressions.' So far as can be gathered from the distinction drawn between them in *or.* II. 54 the English equivalent of *cavillatio* would be 'irony,' of *dicacitas* 'wit in repartee.'

Nihil agens cum republica] The phrase has been much puzzled over by the commentators. It is however admirably explained as follows by Matth. *ad Cic. Cat.* III. 14: *qui a consiliis de rep. se ipse removeat, dicitur nihil agens cum rep., ut resp. per* προσωποποιΐαν *ipsa consilia inire fingatur.*

Nihil (metuas) mali] *Nihil metuas mali* is the reading of most editors, but against the authority of the best MSS. It is moreover quite a needless alteration, for the twofold sense of *sperare* (as in the case of the Greek ἐλπίζειν) makes it a peculiarly suitable word in a construction like the present. Mr Watson has introduced *speres* in the second clause as well, but its repetition is unnecessary and mars the elegance of the ζεῦγμα.

Eius collega] 'His colleague (Messala) is at once most complimentary to me, and an enthusiastic champion of the good cause.'

Quin imo] Schütz, *quin nunc* Matth., either of which is more forcible than *qui nunc*, which it is proposed to substitute for them. 'More by token they are not very good friends just now: and I have my fears that the infection may spread.'

§ 3 *Sed*] Not, I think, 'in spite of Messala's energy,' as Mr Watson understands it, but 'in spite of my satisfaction at their rupture:' for Cicero was glad of the *fact*, but afraid of the *precedent*.

Quod infectum est] It is not to the bad example of Clodius that he alludes, as it is explained by Murctus and others, but to the discord which it was producing, as shewn by the fact that the two consuls took different sides in the question. In his eagerness to prevent an open rupture in the Senate Cicero would probably have dropped the case *in toto*, if the right feeling of Cato and others had not made such a course impossible. As it was, he shewed a want of energy in the matter most discreditable to himself, and no doubt most prejudicial to his influence for good in the state.

Instaurassent] 'After the fresh performance of the sacrifice:' for the first had been polluted by a man's presence. This is the regular sense of *instaurare*, 'to *repeat* a sacrifice,' cf. Liv. V. 19, Verg. *Aen*. III. 62. Occasionally, as in Verg. *Aen*. IV. 145, it means 'to repeat *again and again*.' *Ideoque*, which Schütz has adopted in place of *idque*, though it greatly improves the sentence, can scarcely be called necessary.

Q. Cornificio] He was probably of praetorian rank: cf. *Ep*. I. 1, where he is mentioned as an unsuccessful candidate for the consulship. Even Abeken is not quite satisfied with Cicero's conduct on this occasion, which he criticises as follows: 'He was lukewarm in the performance of the duties devolving on a consular.... In January, 693, Q. Cornificius brought the matter before the Senate. We are surprised that this should not have been done by a senator of more consequence; but Cicero, though he likewise expresses astonishment at the circumstance, did not offer to come forward.'

Nostrum] 'Men of my own standing,' i.e. of consular rank. Why is Cicero so particular to mention this fact? Not, as is commonly suggested, to cast blame on the consulars, himself amongst the number, but because he fancies that Atticus will sanction his irresolute policy in a matter the issues of which were as yet so uncertain.

Nefas] 'Sacrilege.' The *rogatio* in question was to enable a special court of enquiry to be held on the circumstances of the case.

Nuncium remisisse]=*repudiare*, 'to divorce.' *Uxori*, i.e. Pompeia, daughter of Q. Pompeius Rufus. It was at her house that the proceedings had taken place, her husband being Pontifex Maximus at the time.

Operam dat] 'Is straining every nerve to defeat the

measure, although it has been issued in his own name, in obedience moreover to a special decree and on a question of sacrilege. Messala so far is for pressing the matter rigorously.'

Antiquetur] *Antiquare* is used in reference to a measure which is still under consideration: *abrogare*, of an actual law which it is proposed to annul.

Boni viri] i.e. *optimates*: like *bonarum partium* in § 2. The word *operae*, 'ruffians,' 'hirelings,' appears again in *Ep.* 14. 5, *operae Clodianae*.

Lycurgei] In allusion to the Athenian orator of that name, who is mentioned in *Brut.* XXXIV. 130, and also in Diod. XVI. 88, where he is called πικρότατος κατήγορος. 'I myself, though a very Lycurgus at the outset, am daily losing the edge of my wrath.' Yet, in the face of this avowal, Abeken can defend Cicero's inertness on the plea that 'he was not able to take in the whole import of a case at once!'

Qui...fuissemus] The mood (as in *Ep.* 4. 2) presents difficulties to Boot, who would understand it as conditional: *si Clodius statim reus factus esset.* But cf. Madv. 366, obs. 3.

Quid multa?] 'In short I fear that this outrage, neglected as it is by the good, and espoused by the vicious, will prove a fertile source of peril to the state.'

§ 4 *Scin quem dicam?*] Casaubon would extend this parenthesis to include the words *laudare coepisse.* The question is one of little moment, but a comparison with other passages where the phrase occurs is against the proposed alteration.

Amplectitur] The strongest possible word = ἀγαπάζειν, 'takes me to his bosom.' The motives of Pompeius for this display of friendship are admirably given by Casaubon in a very few words: *Serviebat enim omnibus gratiosis tum temporis, ut acta eius bello Mithridatico confirmarentur.*

Nihil come] 'There is no sympathy, no candour, no integrity in his politics: nothing dignified or resolute, or manly.' It is strange that even for a moment Hortensius should have been thought to be the subject of these words, when they so exactly agree with the description given of Pompeius by M. Caelius (*ad div.* VIII. 1. 3), *aliud sentire et loqui, neque tantum valere ingenio ut non appareat quid cupiat,*' and again by Cicero himself in a subsequent letter, *Pompeius fremit, queritur, Scauro studet; sed utrum fronte an mente dubitatur.*

Terrae filio] A man of whose parents and antecedents nothing is known. 'This son of the soil, goodness knows who he is.' (Cf. Pers. VI. 56, *ad div.* VII. 9. 3.) *Subtilius*, 'more in detail.'

§ 5 *Praetores*] Among whom were C. Caesar and Cicero's brother Quintus. The delay in their appointment, as we may infer from *Ep.* 14. 5, was due to the Clodian trial. Cf. *Ep.* 18. 7, where the pressure of home business accounts for a similar postponement.

Includam] This is generally taken to mean 'I'll insert it in my speech.' But, to judge from *Ep.* I. 16. 10, *includere in epistolam* is the usual phrase in that case. Moreover it is an unlikely subject to form part of a speech, nor does it appear in any of those which have come down to us. I should therefore prefer to translate 'I'll send it you with my speech,' i.e. inclose it in the same parcel.

Mendose fuisse] 'I had already perceived that the date was a mistake.' In all probability he refers simply to an earlier letter; rather than to a date given in one of his speeches.

ἀττικώτερα] 'More classical,' with an evident allusion to his friend's name: a joke which he elaborates in the corresponding passage of *Ep.* 19. 10.

Orationem Metellinam] 'My speech against Metellus.' *Orationem habuerat mense ianuario superioris anni contra contionem Q. Metelli Nepotis trib. pl. a quo consulatu abiens pro more verba ad populum facere fuerat prohibitus.* Boot. Only fragments of this speech are extant, collected for the most part from Gell. XVIII. 7.

Liber] 'I will send you a copy, since affection for me has made you such an ardent admirer of rhetoric. Have I anything new to tell you? Anything? Yes.' With the concluding sentences cf. *Ep. ad Quint. fr.* III. 1. 24 *quid praeterea? quid? etiam*, etc.

§ 6 *Autronianam*] i.e. of Lucius Autronius Paetus, who had been twice convicted, first of bribery and afterwards of participation in the conspiracy of Catiline. He was at present in exile (*ad Att* III. 2, *or. pro Sull.* VI.).

HS XXXVII] i.e. *sestertium tricies septies*. It is useless to print the reading of the best MS HS CXXXIV, for (as Casaubon remarks) to give any point to the comparison which follows, we may fairly argue that the house in question was not bought at a cheaper rate than his own. For an account of Cicero's purchase, cf. *Ep. ad div.* V. 6. 2.

Quid id ad me, inquies?] 'You will ask how that affects me? Only in this way, that, as compared with him, I am thought to have made a good bargain, and men begin to understand that a certain distinction is attainable by using a friend's money for a purchase.'

Lentum negocium est] 'Drags its slow length along, but for all that I have hopes of it.' Mr Watson translates the word *negocium* by 'creature' on the analogy of the Greek χρῆμα, but the ordinary explanation appears to me more natural.

Ista confice] *Insta, confice* Schütz, in reference to the business of Τεῦκρις: a reading which is particularly tempting if (as I think) Τεῦκρις is identical with Antonius, whom Atticus was on the point of visiting. But the fact that it settles everything so comfortably is perhaps an argument for rejecting it. Add to which *mandata effice quae recepisti* in § 7 of the next letter is the exact equivalent of *ista* in the present, and in that passage it cannot possibly refer to Τεῦκρις, whose business was by that time settled.

LETTER XIV.

Epitome of Contents] § 1 *His want of leisure. The first speech of Pompeius after his return from the east, and* § 2 *his opinion on the subject of the Clodian scandal.* § 3 *The panegyric of Crassus on Cicero's consulship, and* § 4 *his own speech which followed it.* § 5 *The progress of the Clodian trial.* § 6 *The character of the consuls.* § 7 *His private affairs, e.g. the promise of* Τεῦκρις, *his brother's purchase of a house, and his own relations with Lucceius.*

§ 1] 'I am afraid you will think it affectation in me to tell you how busy I am: but for all that I *am* so worried that I can hardly find time for this brief scrawl.'

Putidum] 'Stale' is the literal sense: from which the word is used figuratively of anything that becomes affected or formal from tedious reiteration. (Cf. *ad div.* VIII. 5, *de off.* I. 37. 133.)

Scripsi ad te antea]· in a letter either lost or purposely destroyed. The allusion in § 4 of the last letter is not definite enough to suit the occasion.

Iucunda miseris] 'The speech was not satisfactory to the poor, nor encouraging to the vicious: to the well-to-do it was unacceptable, to the good frivolous, and so it fell flat.' We may notice in the above the use of the figure *chiasmus*, in which the contrast is between the first and third, 'the poor... the rich,' and again between the second and fourth, 'the turbulent...the well-disposed.' *Frigebat,* 'met with a cold reception.' Cf. *refrixerit* I. 2, and *refrixerat* 19. 4. For the position of Pompeius at the present time, who by disbanding his army had destroyed the secret of his own power, cf. Merivale's *Life of Cicero*, p. 62.

Fufius] Quintus Fufius Calenus, a bitter enemy of Cicero, as we find from the *Philippics* and elsewhere in the orations.

In contionem produxit] 'Introduced Pompeius to the assembly.' It is a note-worthy fact that no one, not even the consuls themselves at the *comitia tributa* (cf. Matth. *ad Sest.* 33), could address the people except by the authority of the magistrates who had convened the meeting.

Circo Flaminio] which was outside the walls of the city, where Pompeius was waiting till a decree should allow him to enter in triumph.

Nundinarum πανήγυρις] 'A conclave of market people,' which would ensure a good attendance at the assembly. There is no doubt an intentional mock solemnity in this use of the word πανήγυρις. Casaubon draws attention to the levity shewn by Fufius in selecting by preference a day which till quite lately had been included among the *dies nefasti*.

Quaesivit ex eo] 'He put the question to him whether he was in favour of the judges being chosen by the praetor on the understanding that he was afterwards to be advised by them in court. For so it had been ordered by the Senate for the trial of the Clodian sacrilege.' This selection of the judges by the praetor on whom the conduct of the case devolved was contrary to the ordinary rule, which provided that they should be chosen by lot, subject to the people's approval. Upon this point everything depended. The praetors would only choose respectable judges; whereas election by lot was a matter of chance, or might give room for corruption. Meriv.

Consilio] Compare the well-known passages in Verg. *Aen.* VI. 430, Prop. V. II. 20. In *Ep.* 16 § 5 we have the phrase *ad consilium refertur*, which means simply that the question was formally referred to the bench.

§ 2 μάλ' ἀριστοκρατικῶς] 'In the spirit of a true aristocrat,' 'in true conservative fashion.'

Maximam] 'Supreme.' Mr Watson reads '*maximi* videri' with Klotz, but I cannot believe that Cicero's ear would have been satisfied with so unpleasant a rhythm.

Promulgata rogatione] 'The bill before the house.'

γενικῶς] It makes little difference whether we translate 'in general terms' with Schütz and Matth., or 'en masse'

with Orelli and others, as in either case the meaning is the
same, that he did not venture to speak definitely against
Clodius, connected as he was with the most influential citizens,
on whose agency he was himself depending for the ratifi-
cation of his acts in Asia.

De istis rebus] is the reading of Schütz, Matth. and the
majority of the editors, while Nobbe gives *istius* 'about the
proceedings of a friend of yours,' i.e. the events of Cicero's
consulship and the punishment of the conspirators. Cf. *Ep.* 16.
13 *istos consulatus non flocci facteon*. It is difficult to decide
between these two readings, which are almost identical in
meaning, as I cannot believe that either the one or the other
can refer simply to the sacrilege and the subsequent trial.
Nostris, which is accepted by Klotz, is in all probability an
explanatory gloss.

§ 3 *Ornatissime*] 'Spoke in most complimentary terms of
my consulship, and even went so far as to say that he owed
to me his life and all that was enjoyable in life.' This panegyric is again referred to in *Ep* 16. 5, where it enables us to
identify Crassus as the subject of the allusion.

Quid multa?] 'In short, the whole of that topic which in
my speeches, of which you are the critic, I paint in hues so
varied, about the fire, the sword—you know the resources
of my colour-boxes—he wove with great dignity into the
thread of his argument.'

Aristarchus] An Alexandrine critic of Homer, whose
severity had passed into a proverb. Cf. *ad div.* III. 11. 5.
Hor. *Ars P.* 450.

ληκύθους] λήκυθοι, or *ampullae*, are literally vessels in which
painters kept their colours, used figuratively of rhetorical
embellishments. Cf. Plin. *Ep.* II. 2 *Marci nostri* ληκύθους
non fugimus, and in particular *Ep. ad Att.* II. 1 *meus autem
liber totum Isocrati* μυροθήκιον *atque omnes eius discipulorum
arculas ac nonnihil etiam Aristotelia pigmenta consumpsit*.

Proxime Pompeium] *Pompeio* Boot and others from a
single MS, but the reading of the text may be readily explained as elliptical for *proxime ad*.

Utrum Crassum inire] A remarkable construction in
place of the more usual *utrum quod Crassus iniret* etc. 'because Crassus was establishing a claim for gratitude.' The
above is a simpler explanation than the one suggested by
Boot: *sive quia videbat Crassum inire gratiam...sive quia
intelligebat tantas esse res nostras*, etc.

Tam libenti senatu] 'With such kindly expressions on the
part of the Senate.'

Perstrictus esset] 'Wounded,' 'roughly handled.' For this use of *perstringere* cf. *Brut.* XCIV. *consulatus meus primo illum leviter perstrinxerat*. The word *litterae* includes his writings of whatever kind, e.g. the speech for the Manilian law (ch. 11), and that for Sestius (ch. 31)—passages which teem with the praises of Pompeius as the conqueror of Spartacus, when the insurrection had been virtually suppressed by Crassus.

§ 4 *Crasso adiunxit*] 'That day has made me the close ally of Crassus.' This compliment on the part of Crassus was well timed, perhaps intentionally so, as by it he disarmed the animosity of Cicero till his designs in reference to the trial had been accomplished.

Aperte tecte] The juxtaposition of these two words has occasioned considerable difficulty, but there is really little doubt that they are to be separated in translation, and were only brought together to heighten the contrast between them, i.e. *quod ille mihi tecte dederat, aperte accepi*. Two other explanations have been proposed: (i) to take them as equivalent to *sive tecte sive aperte*, and (ii) to understand them as an oxymoron: 'with artful candour.'

Ego autem ipse] 'For myself, great Heaven! how I did flare up for the benefit of my new pupil, Pompeius. If ever periods, or turns, or syllogisms, or flourishes came at my call, they certainly did so then. In short I brought the house down. For this was my theme: the dignity of our order, and its harmony with the knights, the unity of Italy, the dying embers of the conspiracy, the cheapness of provisions, the prevailing peace. You know by experience what my thunders are on topics like these: so loud were they on this occasion that I may be brief, for I think they must have reached you even across the water.'

ἐνεπερπερευσάμην] 'How I did shew off,' a ἅπαξ λεγόμενον in classical writings, although it occurs in Epictetus and in the *Ep. ad Corinth.* I. xiii. 4 ἡ ἀγάπη οὐ περπερεύεται. Κατεπείρεται is the gloss of Hesychius, and the word πέρπερος is described as equivalent to ἀλαζών.

ἐνθυμήματα] *Rhetorical syllogisms*: while κατασκευαί according to Gronovius and Schütz are *figurae elocutionis*. Ernesti on the other hand regards the word as equivalent to *confirmationes, constructive* as opposed to *destructive* arguments (ἀνασκευαί). Mr Watson still edits καρποί in place of καμπαί, but the latter has been received as a certain emendation by Schütz, Matth. and others.

Intermortuis] The emendation of Ernesti, which is accepted by the majority of the editors, but *immortuis* 'nipped in the bud' is the reading of the MS, and gives a more forcible rendering, as the writer does not wish to draw special attention to the fact that the conspiracy still lives.

Vilitate] *annonae*. For the omission cf. *or. Verr.* III. 93. 216 *biennium provinciam obtinuit, quum alter annus in vilitate, alter in summa caritate fuerit.* Mr Watson draws attention to the fact that this cheapness of provisions was probably due to the appointment of Pompeius as *praefectus annonae*, which had been made at Cicero's suggestion in the year 63 B.C.

§ 5] 'As for the position of affairs at Rome, the Senate is a very Areopagus. No council was ever more resolute, stern or consistent. For when the day came for submitting the senatorial measure to the people, bearded boys came trooping up—the whole of Catiline's herd—with Curio's slip of a girl at their head, and entreated the people to reject the bill. Even Piso the consul, who had proposed the measure, now raised his voice against it. The hirelings of Clodius had beset the gangways, and the voting tickets were being supplied in such a way that no applicant received an Aye. On this you should have seen Cato fly to the platform and deliver himself of a marvellous invective against Piso, if one may use the word of an utterance that breathed dignity and determination, aye, and the salvation of our cause. Our friend Hortensius followed suit, and after him many good men and true. Favonius too did us good service.'

Concursabant] To '*run to and fro*' in an eager and excited way rather than to '*crowd together*' is the precise meaning of *concursare*. Cf. the Greek περιπατεῖν.

Barbatuli iuvenes] The diminutive expresses his contempt for their youth—it may be also for their foppishness. Cf. τὴν δ' ὑπήνην ἄκουρον τρέφων as the mark of a dandy in Aristoph. *Vesp.* 477. In the *or. in Cat.* II. 22 he describes the followers of Catiline as *pexo capillo nitidos aut imberbes aut bene barbatos*.

Filiola Curionis] i.e. Caius Scribonius Curio. Cf. *Phil.* II. 18. In Vell. Pat. II. 48. 3 he is described as *vir nobilis, eloquens, audax, suae alienaeque et fortunae et pudicitiae prodigus*.

Idem] Cf. XI. 1 *nunc idem videar diffidere*, and the note on the passage.

Pontes] The gangways or approaches by which the citizens passed to the 'septa,' where they assembled by their tribes or centuries, and out of which they passed to give their votes.

For a full description of the method of voting, cf. Mr Forsyth's *Life of Cic.* p. 94.

Tabellae] These were tickets, two of which were given to each voter, one of them inscribed with the letters A. P. (*antiqua probo*) or A (*antiquo*), the other with the letters V. R. (*uti rogas*).

Salutis] is sometimes taken to mean 'sound advice,' but this translation does not make the climax sufficiently strong, especially after the words *gravitas* and *auctoritas*.

Favonii] From the *or. pro Mil.* IX. 26 he seems in most things to have followed the lead of Cato, whose principles he shared. Cf. also *ad div.* VIII. 11. 2. He was put to death after the battle of Philippi.

Quum decerneretur] 'When the moment came for passing the decree.' *Nullum facienti* i.e. *faciendum censenti*, 'who was for passing no decree on the subject.' Boot confuses the present decree 'ut consules populum cohortarentur' with the earlier one for the appointment of a court of enquiry when he translates the passage thus: 'who was for cancelling the decree on the subject.'

Curioni] The elder Curio is meant, as the son was not of age to be on the roll of the Senate—a fact which is sufficiently established by the use of the word *introductus* in *ad Att.* II. 24. 3.

Fufius tribunus tum concessit] *Fufius territus concessit* Gron., of which Boot approves on the ground that the addition of *tribunus* is otiose after the mention of his rank in the earlier portion of the letter. But it was important to reassert his official capacity on an occasion like the present: while the reading of the MSS *tertium* is more nearly represented by *tri. tum* than by *territus*.

Contiones miseras] 'Clodius delivered himself of some pitiful harangues in which he assailed Lucullus, Hortensius, Piso and Messala with foul abuse: all he laid to my charge was that I had brought his deeds to light.'

Tantum comperisse omnia] In allusion to Cicero's tedious reiteration of his services in the detection of the Catilinarian conspiracy [cf. *ad div.* V. 5]. But there is a farther sarcasm in the word *tantum* on his want of energy in the conduct of the Clodian prosecution: 'that I had brought his deeds to light, and nothing more,' i.e. had detected but not helped to punish them.

Legationibus] Not the 'appointment of colonial governors,' but the 'reception of foreign ambassadors,' for which

NOTES. 87

the month of February was specially reserved by the Gabinian law. Cf. *Ep.* 18. 7 *quare etiam legationes reiectum iri puto: Ep. ad div.* I. 4. 1, and *ad Q. Fratr.* II. 13. 3.

Lata esset] 'Till the bill has become law.'

§ 6] 'So much for Roman politics: but let me tell you further a piece of news for which I was not prepared. The consul Messala is a fine fellow: resolute, consistent, energetic: add to which he praises, admires and imitates your humble servant. His colleague is saved from being utterly vicious by the possession of one vice, his sleepiness, ignorance and general incapacity: but for all that he is so ill-conditioned in temper that he has hated Pompeius ever since he praised the Senate in his speech.'

Ille alter] Marcus Piso. For the construction *uno vitio minus vitiosus* Boot compares Ov. *Metam.* XII. 554 *Bis sex Herculeis ceciderunt, nec minus uno Viribus.*

ἀπρακτότατος] Like ἀπράγμων, 'unpractical.' Casaubon notices κακέκτης as a medical term to denote a man with a bad habit of body. Hence the addition of *voluntate*.

Cornuto] Caius Cornutus, who three years later was elected praetor.

Pseudo-Catone] Not 'Cornutus is a true pseudo-Cato,' as it has been proposed to render it, but 'Cornutus, believe me, is a second Cato.' The use of *bonis* in the context is decisive against our understanding the words in a disparaging sense.

Quid quaeris?] 'Have I told you everything?' A formula which denotes not so much surprise on the part of the questioner as a farther desire for information. But the phrase is so unusual in this sense and in this position, that, as Casaubon suggests, a sentence may possibly have been lost. Boot's re-arrangement of the text is hardly a success: *Bonis utimur tribunis plebis, Cornuto vero—quid quaeris?—Pseudo-Catone.*

§ 7 *Quae recepisti*] 'Attend to the commissions which you have undertaken.' Cf. *ista* in § 6 of the preceding letter.

Argiletani] A part of Rome near the Palatine, so called from the beds of clay (*argilla*) in the neighbourhood.

The derivation from *Argi letum* (Serv. *ad Aen.* VIII. 341) is purely fanciful, though it has been perpetuated by Martial in the well-known line *Argi nempe soles subire letum*. [*Epigr.* I. 118. 9.]

Reliquum dodrantem] 'The remaining three-fourths.' Quintus had probably been mentioned in the will as *haeres ex quadrante*, and afterwards purchased the remainder of the house from his co-legatees. *Venditat*, 'is trying to dispose of.'

In gratiam redi] 'Make it up with Lucceius. I see he is labouring under a sharp touch of office fever. I will do my best for him.' The word *petiturire* is admirably illustrated by *Ep.* 17. 11 *Lucceium scito consulatum habere in animo statim petere*, and it is surprising that any editor should be in favour of rewriting the sentence so as to make it form part of the preceding.

LETTER XV.

Epitome of Contents] § 1 *The assignment of the province of Asia Minor to his brother Quintus, and his hope that it may add to the reputation of the family.* § 2 *The correspondence between them.*

§ 1 *Asiam*] This was one of the most coveted of the praetorian provinces, and included Ionia, Caria, Phrygia and Lydia.

φιλέλληνες] Cf. the *Or. pro Flacco* cap. XIV. and elsewhere.

παντοίης ἀρετῆς μιμνήσκεο] *Il.* XXII. 268. He expected at this time that Atticus would go into Asia as one of his brother's retinue, but he afterwards gave up the intention. Cf. *Ep.* 16. 14 *quod ad me scribis te in Asiam statuisse non ire, equidem mallem ut ires, et vereor ne quid in ista re minus commode fiat.*

§ 2 *De tuo negocio*] The Sicyonian debt, in all probability.

LETTER XVI.

Epitome of Contents] § 1 *A plea for his conduct in the matter of the Clodian trial, and more particularly* § 2 *in reference to the measure of Hortensius.* §§ 3—5 *The progress and issue of the trial.* § 6 *Affairs at Rome.* § 7 *His hopes for the future.* §§ 8, 9 *His speeches after the verdict.* § 10 *His passage of arms with Clodius.* § 11 *His present position in the state.* § 12 *The coming consular election.* § 13 *The new laws against bribery.* § 14 *The projected visit of Atticus to Asia Minor.* § 15 *On literary subjects, and* § 16 *his own correspondence.* § 17 *The private affairs of Atticus, and* § 18 *his Amaltheum in Epirus.*

§ 1] 'You ask me what can have happened on the trial to result in such an extraordinary verdict: also why I fought less brilliantly than is my wont. I will answer your last question first after the fashion of Homer. To tell the truth, so long as I could plead the resolution of the Senate, I fought with might and main, insomuch that applause and rallyings ensued to my great honour. Nay, if ever you have thought me bold to protect the state, most assuredly you would have done so then. For when I found he had taken refuge in mob-meetings and was holding up my name to scorn, great Heavens! what fight I shewed, what havoc I dealt! what onslaughts I made on Piso, Curio and the whole of their crew! How bitterly I inveighed against the frivolity of the old men, the licentiousness of the young! Often, so help me Heaven! I longed for you not only to advise me in my counsels, but to be the eyewitness of my marvellous prowess.'

Quaeris ex me] The question proves that Atticus misdoubted his friend's sincerity on the occasion, although he did not fathom his motives. The answer of Cicero shews that his energy in the prosecution was confined to vague declamation, while for abandoning the key of the position he offers no defence at all—for *contraxi vela perspiciens inopiam iudicum* is none.

ὕστερον πρότερον] *praepostere.* Thus Homer begins the tale of Troy in the 9th year, and gives us the history of the previous period in his later narrative. So again in the *Odyssey* he begins with the 10th year of the wanderings of Ulysses, which finds him in the island of Calypso, and fills in his earlier history by episodes in the succeeding books.

Auctoritas] The resolution mentioned in § 1 of *Ep.* 14, *iudices a praetore legi quo consilio idem praetor uteretur.*

Ad invidiam uteretur] As a traitor to the popular cause in the opposition which he had offered to the Agrarian schemes of Rullus, and in the illegal punishment of the Catilinarian conspirators.

§ 2 *Hortensius excogitavit*] Fufius, as Casaubon remarks, was no doubt the crafty originator of this scheme, and had in all probability suggested it to Hortensius as the readiest means of proceeding with the case. Hortensius was perhaps honest in his belief that an ordinary bench of judges would secure a conviction; or else, like Cicero, he was not unwilling that the criminal should escape, so long as he could explain satisfactorily his own part in the matter.

Inopiam iudicum] like *egestas* below, the neediness and poverty of the judges.

Pro testimonio] As for instance that Clodius was at Rome at the time of the sacrilege and not at Interamna, as he had pretended. (Cf. *Ep.* II. 1. 5. Plut. *Cic.* 29.)

Commissum est] 'For this result we are indebted to the rash counsels of Hortensius, who, in his fear that Fufius would put his veto upon the senatorial measure, never saw how far wiser it had been to leave the criminal in his ignominy and disgrace than to trust for his conviction to a weak bench of judges.'

Dum veritus est] For this rare use of *dum* with a past tense to denote duration of time, cf. Zumpt, § lxxvi. pp. 355, 356, and the *Public School Lat. Gr.* p. 162, I. 6.

Tamen] For this common elliptical use of *tamen* cf. *Ep.* 19. 8 *atque ita tamen his novis amicitiis implicati sumus*, and Ellendt, *ad orat.* V. 2, p. 208, 'that a sword, were it of lead, would yet suffice to cut his throat.' The proverb appears again in *de fin.* IV. 18. 48.

§ 3 *Incredibili exitu*] 'The result passes all belief: so that now, when all is over, everyone else blames the scheme of Hortensius, as I have done from the first.'

Reiectio] For this challenging of the judges, cf. the *locus classicus* on the subject, *Verr.* I. 6. 16, and the comments of Asconius upon it.

Accusator] Lucius Lentulus (Plut. *in Caes.* 10), who was consul with Caius Marcellus in the year 705. Among the *subscriptores* to the prosecution were two relatives of Lentulus, and also Caius Fannius (*ad Att.* II. 24. 3).

Tanquam clemens lanista] who, in selecting the pairs of combatants for the games, would naturally choose the most worthless for the arena and retain the more respectable for use in the training school.

Consederunt] 'As soon as ever the jury were empanelled, good men began to entertain strong doubts. For a more rascally lot never sat round a gaming table. Degraded senators were there, and beggarly knights, and tribunes cashiered rather than rich in cash. Yet were they interspersed with a few good men of whom the criminal couldn't rid himself by the exercise of the challenge. These sat sad and sorrowful among companions so unlike themselves, and were sorely troubled by their close contact with such villains.'

Maculosi] There is some doubt whether this word is to be taken in a general sense of men of tarnished reputation (*infamiae maculis conspersi*, Tac. *Ann.* XIII. 33, *Hist.* I. 7), or as referring definitely to the *nota* or *macula censoria* (cf. Suet. *Iul.* 41). The latter is more forcible and indeed necessary, if, as I am inclined to believe, each of the adjectives represents some formal sentence of disgrace.

Nudi] 'Beggared,' 'threadbare in money and reputation,' is the usual explanation; but, on the principle mentioned above, I believe it refers definitely to the loss of their ring—the bitterest disgrace with which an *eques* could be visited.

Aerati...aerarii] *Tribuni aerarii sunt ordinis plebeii* (*or. pro Planc.* V.) *et per eos militibus pecunia stipendiorum numerabatur, ut est auctor Festus.* Ern. In accordance with the above Muretus has proposed a rearrangement of the passage, which is certainly ingenious: *Tribuni non tam aerarii, ut appellantur, quam aerati.* 'Tribunes not so much *paymasters* as *receivers of pay*.' But this premature suggestion of *bribery* is quite foreign to the tone of the narrative, and it is to the antecedents of the jurymen rather than to their conduct on this occasion that the sarcasms evidently refer. Rejecting therefore any explanation which would find a direct allusion to bribery in the passage I should understand it somewhat in the sense of *maculosi* above. Cf. *Cluent*. 43 *in aerarios referri*, i.e. *in ultimam classem, cui ascripti suffragio carebant, et tantum aera tributi loco pendebant. erat autem haec nota censoria, quam plebi quidem in primis, sed interdum tamen etiam senatoribus et equitibus inurebant.* Ern.

§ 4 *Consilium*] *Iuris peritorum qui praetori assidebant*, Matth., but the words which follow prove conclusively that the judges themselves are meant.

Primis postulationibus] 'As each point was submitted to the bench on the first hearing:' a very similar process to the Greek ἀνάκρισις. Originally *postulatio* meant no more than to ask the praetor's leave for permission to lodge the suit: but it had been extended to include all the details upon which the contending parties might require information before the actual trial of the suit commenced.

Triumphavit] 'In a word Hortensius was in ecstacies at his own foresight.'

Ex acclamatione] The order is *audisse ex acclamatione*, 'I think the uproar must have been loud enough to tell you,' and for the hyperbola compare the precisely similar expression *usque istim exauditos* in *Ep.* 14. 4. It has been strangely enough proposed to contort the sentence into the following form: *credo te audisse quae consurrectio facta sit ex acclamatione*, 'how the jury rose as one man on hearing the outcry raised by the partisans of Clodius.' It may be noticed in passing that *acclamatio* in Cicero always denotes *disapprobation:* differing in this from the similar compound *admurmurare*, which is likewise used in a favourable sense. Cf. *in Pis.* XIV. 31. On the subject of *advocatus* it is scarcely necessary to warn even schoolboys against translating it 'an advocate' or 'counsel.' It is really no more than a friend, called in by either party to watch the case, and, if need be, to give evidence in his favour.

Honorificentior] 'More complimentary.' *Tui cives*, i. e. *Athenienses*. As a matter of fact they were not the fellow-citizens of Atticus, as he had declined the offer of their franchise, because by receiving it he would have lost his position as a citizen of Rome. Cf. *quum ex nostro iure duarum civitatum nemo esse possit.* [Cic. *pro Caec.* XXXIV. 100.]

Xenocratem] of Chalcedon, a pupil of Plato and the fellow-student of Aristotle. The story to which he alludes is told by Diog. Laert. (IV. 7), and is repeated by Cicero in the *or. pro Balbo*, cap. V. 12, though on that occasion he gives the circumstances only without mentioning the name.

Tabulas] 'That occasion on which a Roman jury declined to inspect the account-books of Metellus, when as usual they were being carried round for inspection: far greater, I repeat, was the compliment in my own case.' The circumstance occurred during the trial of Metellus for peculation, and is mentioned again in the *or. pro Balbo*, cap. V. 11.

§ 5] 'And so by the expressions of the jurymen, for I was hailed by them as the saviour of my country, the defendant was crushed, and with him fell all his supporters, while at my house the day after I was met by as great a concourse as that by which I was escorted home at the close of my consulship. Our immaculate Areopagites protested that they could not make their way to court except under the protection of a guard. It was referred to the bench. One voice alone was raised against the appointment of a guard. So the question was laid before the Senate, and the guard voted in most impressive and complimentary terms: the judges praised to the skies: the details entrusted to the magistrates: no one thought it possible that the fellow would shew himself in court.'

Convenit] The addition of *postridie* and *venturos* leaves no doubt as to the meaning of this passage. Otherwise 'rallied round me' to accompany me home is the translation which the context would rather suggest.

Abiens consulatu] The occasion is thus referred to in the *or. in Pis., quo quidem tempore is meus domum fuit e foro reditus, ut nemo, nisi qui mecum esset, civium esse in numero videretur.*

Refertur ad consilium] See note on § 4. The quotation which follows is from Hom. *Il.* II. 112, 113.

Calvum] M. Licinius Crassus is meant, as a comparison

with *Ep.* 14. 3 sufficiently proves. That his character was in accordance with the act we may gather from Cic. *de off.* I. 109, and the following passage from Sall. *Cat.* 48, *ne Crassus more suo suscepto malorum patrocinio rem publicam conturbaret.* The only attempt to explain the title 'Calvus, one of the Nanneian set' is offered by Manutius, who suggests that he may have bought the estates of Nanneius (one of those who suffered in the proscriptions of Sulla, cf. Q. Cic. *de pet. cons.* 2) under the feigned name of Calvus, or by the agency of a procurator of that name. Or again it is possible that in the word *calvus* there may be an allusion to his personal appearance, just as in the first satire of Persius the same adjective is descriptive of Nero. As an example of reckless emendation the reading proposed by Boot is unrivalled: *nosti Calvum, ἐξαπιναῖον illum laudatorem meum.*

Intercessit] Cf. *ad Att.* VI. 1. 5 *intercessisse se pro iis magnam pecuniam,* and again *Phil.* II. 45 *sestertium sexagies se pro te intercessisse dicebat.* 'In two days by the aid of a single slave fetched from a training school the business was done: he had seen the judges: promised, guaranteed, and paid the bribe.'

Iam vero] 'To crown it all,' in reference to the *mercedis cumulo* (*auctuarium,* ἐπίμετρον).

Summo discessu bonorum] 'And so, in a court full of slaves, where every good man was conspicuous by his absence, five-and-twenty of the judges were yet so resolute in the hour of danger as to prefer death to the desertion of their post. Thirty-one there were with whom hunger carried the day against honour. Catulus, on encountering one of the latter, said: *What did you want guards for? Was it for fear of being robbed of the wages of your shame?*'

Perdere omnia] is explained by Manutius and others to mean the ruin of the state rather than of their own reputation. I am inclined myself to understand it in the latter sense, 'preferred loss of life to the loss of all that makes life endurable.'

Catulus] The story is told by Plutarch in his life of Cicero, cap. XXIX.

§ 6] 'You have received, in as few words as I can give it, an account of the trial, and the cause of the acquittal. In your next question you ask what is the present position of the Republic and of myself. Let me tell you that the State which you believed to be secured by my care, and I by the care of the gods, and which did appear to be established on a firm basis by the union of all the well-disposed, and by the vigorous measures of my Consulate, has, unless some god looks down on us with mercy, already slipped from our hands by this one judgment—if that can be called a judgment, when thirty men, the most frivolous and abandoned of the Roman people, violate for a paltry bribe every right human and divine; when a Thalna, a Plautus, a Spongia, and other refuse like these, maintain that a deed was not committed which all men, aye and the very brutes themselves, know to a certainty was committed. But yet for your consolation let me tell you, that, although the state has received this heavy blow, still villainy is not so wantonly triumphant in the hour of victory as the vicious had anticipated. For they thought that if religion, chastity, the honour of the judges, and the authority of the Senate, could be overturned, then recklessness and lust might openly revenge themselves on the good among us, for the pain my austere administration had inflicted on the bad.' *Meriv.*

Elapsum de manibus] He uses the same expression of a trial in the *de orat.* II. 50. 202 *nihil unquam vidi, quod tam e manibus elaberetur, quam mihi tum est elapsa illa causa.*

Thalnam et Plautum et Spongiam] Contemptuous names adopted for the occasion from the lowest class of slaves. The derivations to which Casaubon would refer each of these words are, excepting as regards Spongia, very farfetched. It is surely enough to suppose that in many cases, though by no means in all, the name of a slave had reference to his occupation. Thus *Spongia* is almost precisely identical with *Peniculus*, the name of the parasite who plays so important a part in the Menaechmi: and again in Propertius we have the line *Deliciaeque meae Latris cui nomen ab usu est* (V. 7. 75). But to attempt to find a special allusion of the same kind in so common a word as *Plautus* is surely somewhat fanciful.

Quisquilias] συρφετός, the sweepings of a stable. He uses the same word of the same class in his speech *pro Sestio*, in which he calls Numerius, Serranus and Aelius 'quisquiliae seditionis Clodianae.'

§ 7 *Doloris quem...inusserat*] a favourite phrase with our author; cf. *or. in Verr.* II. 1. 44 *cur hunc dolorem cineri eius atque ossibus inussisti?* and again *or. pro Mil.* XXXVI. *nullum mihi tantum dolorem inuretis;* and again *Phil.* XI. 15. 38 *tertio generi...cupio quam acerbissimum dolorem inurere.*

§ 8 *Ab aliis legi* A reading which Klotz has introduced into his text, and to which Madvig (*ad fin.* p. 29) gives a qualified approval. For *aliis legi* cf. *ad Att.* XVI. 13 a. 1. For the sentiment Matth. compares *ad div.* XV. 21. 5 *aliter enim scribimus quod eos solos quibus mittimus, aliter quod multos lecturos putamus.*

Recreavi] 'It was I who gave fresh courage to the good who were cast down by reassuring them and rousing them to action; while by attacking and worrying these venal jurymen I shut the mouths of all who gloried in his triumph. To Piso the consul I allowed no resting-place for the sole of his foot. He had been promised Syria, but I took it from him. In a word, I restored the Senate to its ancient vigour, revived the despairing, and annihilated Clodius to his face in the Senate by a continuous and most dignified harangue, no less than by a passage of arms, of which I may treat you to a few tit bits, for the rest can have neither pith nor point apart from the heat of the action which you Greeks call ἀγών.'

Nulla in re consistere] A metaphor from an army which is driven from place to place by the enemy, with no time allowed it to organize a resistance. Cf. *patria Turnum consistere terra*. [Verg. *Aen*. X. 75.]

Desponsam] Cf. *de prov. cons*. XV. 37 where the irregular *desponsio* is contrasted with the more formal *decretum*. Mr Watson also notices the fact, that to avoid favouritism it was usual to assign the provinces to the consuls of each year before their election took place. Syria and Macedonia were the most desirable of the consular provinces, and were bestowed as marks of special favour. For instance, the former was promised to Gabinius by Clodius when they made their guilty compact to secure the banishment of Cicero.

Oratione perpetua] λέξις εἰρομένη. It is often used of a set speech as opposed to a railing-match like the one which follows. Vid. Drakenb. *ad Liv*. IV. 6. 1.

§ 9 *De summa republica*] 'The interests of the State.' That *summa respublica*, and not *summa reipublicae*, is the proper form of the phrase is well argued by Zumpt, *ad Verr. L*. II. 28.

Divinitus] 'by inspiration.' The distinction drawn by Casaubon between *divine* and *divinitus: Qui ait se aliquid divine fecisse tribuit sibi laudem: qui dicit divinitus se aliquid egisse laudem deo tribuit non sibi:* is unquestionably a real one, nor is it disproved by the passages quoted by Schütz from the *de orat*. II. 2, II. 45, or by another to which Boot refers in the *Ep. ad Att*. II. 21. 6 *Pompeius loquitur divinitus*, where it may fairly be rendered 'Pompeius talks like one inspired.'

Lentulum] P. Lentulus Sura, the accomplice of Catiline. He had been twice tried for peculation. [Plut. *Cic*. XVII].

Bis Catilinam] Manutius has a long note in proof that Catiline was acquitted in *three* prosecutions: (1) for the seduction of Fabia, a vestal virgin, (2) for the murder of Gratidianus, (3) for malversation in his province. For the omission of the first in the present instance he accounts by the fact that Fabia was the sister of Terentia, and that Cicero had always maintained her innocence of the crime. It would be absurd therefore to refer to the prosecution as evidence of Catiline's guilt.

Immissum] *immittere* is the Greek ἐφιέναι, 'to slip dogs from a leash.' Cf. Verg. *Georg.* III. 351.

Exsilio privare] Cf. *fragm. or. in toga cand.* IV. p. 942 (Orell. ed.) *ad aliquod severius iudicium ac maius supplicium reservari*, and also a remarkable chapter in the *or. pro Caecina*, where it is again mentioned as the more lenient of two alternatives (*or. pro Caec.* XXXIV. 100).

§ 10 *Pulchellus puer*] 'My pretty boy gets up and taunts me with having been at Baiae. A lie, I answer, but what if it were true? no worse than for you to say you had been present at a mystery. 'What,' he continued, 'should a man of Arpinum know of hot baths?' Said I, Tell that tale to your protector, who had a strong fancy for the waters of Arpinum. (You know the stories afloat about the baths of Marius.) 'How long,' he asks, 'shall we stand the airs of this great man?' What! you to talk of a great man, when your great man said nothing about you! (for in his mind's eye he had made short work of the property of his brother-in-law Rex). 'You have bought,' he said, 'a princely mansion.' Yes: but not the judges. 'Your evidence on oath,' said he, 'received no credit.' Indeed it did, was my reply, at least, from five-and-twenty of the judges: the remaining thirty one, seeing they were paid in advance, would clearly give you none. By the shouts which arose he was crushed, silenced and confounded.'

Pulchellus puer] Cf. *ad Att.* II. 1. 4. For a repetition of this sarcasm on his family name we may compare a fragment of the speech against Clodius and Curio (v. ed. Nobbe), *sed, credo, postquam speculum tibi adlatum est, longe te a pulchris abesse sensisti.*

Ad Baias fuisse] A sign of luxury and effeminacy, as it implies the use of the hot bath. Cf. *or. in Clod. et Cur.* IV. sqq., which furnishes a running comment on the passage before us. *Primum homo durus ac priscus invectus est in eos qui mense Aprili apud Baias essent et aquis calidis uterentur. quid cum hoc homine nobis tam tristi et severo?*

Falsum] Schütz rewrites the passage in this form: *sal-*

sum, sed tam id quidem huic simile est, inquam, the weakness of which it is surely needless to demonstrate.

Sed tamen quid hoc?] Why Boot should regard these words as either a gloss or an epistolary comment on the taunt of Clodius, I am at a loss to conceive. They are at any rate forcible enough as a part of Cicero's reply.

In operto fuisse] Cf. *Parad.* IV. 32 *si in opertum Bonae Deae accessisses.* The subject is obscure, but, as the allusion is plain, it is of little real importance whether we supply *te*, which I think makes the retort more forcible: or *me*, with Boot and others. Or again it may be more general still: 'It's no worse than saying one has been in an out-of-the-way place.'

Homini Arpinati] i.e. *agresti ac rustico* (*in Clod. et Cur. ibid.*). For the taunt implied in *aquis calidis*, compare the well-known discussion in the *Clouds* of Aristophanes, 1045 sqq.

Narra patrono tuo] Cf. *narra apud novercam*, Plaut. *Pseud.* I. 3. 80.

Marianas] Matth., *marinas* Schütz and others, a reading which we may unhesitatingly reject, as it rests on little authority and alludes to a doubtful story, which, if true, can have no possible connection with the matter in hand. It seems equally clear that we must understand *aquas* and not *aedes* with the adjective *Marianas:* as, even supposing the latter word could in any case be supplied, it would be next to impossible to do so in the present instance where we have another subject mentioned in such close proximity. We may infer therefore that the allusion is to some spring or baths in the neighbourhood of Arpinum: and the taunt may be simply aimed at the devotion shewn by Clodius to the interests of Marius. But a sarcasm of this kind is not forcible enough to suit the occasion, and it is far more probable that by the word *patronus* some person is meant with whom Clodius was on the same terms as those which existed between the younger Curio and Antonius (*Phil.* II. 18). It has been suggested that the elder Curio may be the person in question, but, although he had warmly supported the cause of Clodius, his character and reputation render it most improbable that he should have been made the subject of a taunt, the import of which can scarcely be mistaken. On the other hand, everything points to the younger Curio as the *patronus* of the text, e.g. his well-known character and the fact that notably on one occasion he acted as the champion of Clodius (*duce filiola Curionis, Ep.* 14. 5), while his father is known to have purchased a house in the neighbourhood of Arpinum which had originally been in the possession of Marius.

One other theory is worthy of notice if only from the fact that it is countenanced by Schütz, viz. that by *patronus* the sister of Clodius is meant, and that her discreditable partiality for Cicero is the subject of the allusion, *Arpinates aquas concupivit*. Against this interpretation we must place the unusual use of the word *patronus*, the apparent want of force in the addition of *Marianas*, and the general tone of the fragmentary speech against Clodius and Curio.

Regem feremus] So again we have *regnum Ciceronis* in the *or. pro Sull.* VII. 21.

Rex] Q. Marcius Rex, the husband of Clodius' sister, Terentia, who had died and left him nothing. For *spe devoraverat* cf. *or. pro dom.* XXIII. 60, and the following from *or. in Verr.* II. 1. 51 *iste qui iam spe atque opinione praedam illam devorasset*.

Domum] A 'mansion,' which is the regular sense of the word in Martial. It would have been natural to refer this to Cicero's house on the Palatine, noticed in *Ep.* 13. 6. However, in the speech already quoted against Clodius and Curio, Cicero implies that a house at *Baiae* is meant and represents himself as commenting thus: *is me dixit aedificare: ubi nihil habeo, ibi fuisse*.

Potes, inquam, dicere, 'iudices emisti?'] The reading of Schütz, with the exception that he omits the interrogative and introduces the negative before *potes*. 'Yes: but can you say I bought the judges?' *Putes, inquam, dicere* is the other reading, which is understood by Boot in the sense of *simile est quasi dicas* above, and by the other editors as equivalent to *facile quispiam putet*. But the taunt in either case becomes less direct and loses in consequence much of its force. *Emisse* for *emisti* suggests itself as a possible emendation. 'Yes, and you can say you bought the judges.'

§ 11 *Missus est sanguis*] 'I have been bled for unpopularity without feeling the smart,' or, in other words, 'The fever of jealousy under which I was labouring has been reduced by bloodletting.' The same idea is found in the speech of Appius (*Liv.* III. 54) *dandus invidiae est sanguis*, in Cic. *ad Att.* VI. 1. 2, and *or. pro Sest.* 38 *sensit suum sanguinem quaeri ad restinguendam invidiam facinoris Clodiani*.

In passing we may call attention to the self-complacency with which Cicero dwells upon the increase of his own popularity at the expense of a blow which he admits to have been well-nigh ruinous to the best interests of the State.

Atque etiam hoc magis] These words are generally understood as an amplification of *sine dolore*: but it is, I think, preferable to regard the passage *missus est sanguis invidiae sine dolore* as parenthetical, and the words in question as a continuation of the sentence *videri nostrum testimonium non valuisse*. We have then the second clause introduced in a natural way by the phrase *accedit quod*, etc.

Rem manifestam] Boot suggests that *reum manifestum illum* is the true reading, and supports it by the parallel passage from *or. pro Mil.* 87 *pecunia se a iudicibus palam redemerat*. There is certainly something very unusual, though at the same time not inexplicable, in the phrase *rem redimere a iudicibus:* moreover, *res* and *reus* are repeatedly confounded in the MSS. Cf. Drakenb. *ad Liv.* XIV. 37. 8.

Contionalis hirudo aerarii] Cf. *ad Quint. fr.* II. 3. 4 *contionario illo populo*. 'Add to which that mob-loving leech of the treasury, a wretched and half-starved rabble, have an idea that I am dearly loved by Pompeius the Great.' The words *hirudo aerarii* account for the increase of his own popularity in consequence of this belief, as it was on Pompeius that their chief hopes of largess depended.

Comissatores coniurationis] 'Our jovial crew of conspirators' (cf. *in Cat.* II. 5. 10), a translation which I much prefer to the more elaborate explanation of Gronovius: *qui inter vinum de coniuratione egerunt*, 'those young friends of ours who play at conspiracy over their cups?' a sense which he illustrates from Curt. VII. 4, *Bessus circumferri merum largius iussit, debellaturus super mensam Alexandrum*.

Ludis et gladiatoribus] 'And so at the plays and gladiatorial shows we won golden favours without the accompaniment of a single hiss.' The word ἐπισημασία is used technically of voting, and in the more general sense is not confined to marks of *favour*, as in the passage before us.

For *pastoricia fistula*, 'shepherds' music,' cf. Plat. *de leg.* III. 700 C, οὐ σύριγξ ἦν οὐδέ τινες ἄμουσοι βοαὶ πλήθους.

§ 12] 'At present we are looking forward anxiously to the elections, in the prospect of which my friend Pompeius is, in spite of all opposition, bringing the son of Aulus to the fore.' By *Auli filium*, as in *Ep.* I. I, Lucius Afranius is meant, whose election was secured by Pompeius. For the sarcasm implied by the omission of his name vid. note on the former passage. Casaubon however suggests that it may have been omitted in imitation of the Greek construction ὁ Ἀρίστωνος, or else to avoid identification, should the letter be intercepted.

In quae] Boot, as usual, would omit altogether this explanatory clause, *in quae modo asellus onustus auro posset ascendere*, as derogatory to the intelligence of Atticus.

For the allusion to Philip, cf. Plut. *apoph. reg.* VIII. p. 96, and Hor. *od.* III. 16. That the same agency was employed by Pompeius is noticed in his life by Plutarch, ch. 44; and again in *Ep. ad Att.* II. 3. 1, *et Epicratem suspicor, ut scribis, lascivum fuisse,* i.e. 'was free with his money.'

Doterionis histrionis similis] al. *deterioris.* When all is said, the allusion in these words is still only imperfectly solved. The reading *deterioris* (which it is attempted to explain by *vv.* 67. sqq. of the Prologue to the *Amphitryon* of Plautus) is now rejected by the best editors, who in the word Doterio—a dispenser of bribes—see a parallel drawn between the consul Piso (*facie magis quam facetiis ridiculus*) and the actors Aristodemus and Neoptolemus, of whom Philip made frequent use in administrating his affairs.

Domitio] L. D. Ahenobarbus, the brother-in-law of Cato.

Apud magistratus] 'The first that a commission of enquiry shall be held before the proper authorities : the other that any person at whose house bribery agents are entertained shall be held guilty of a state offence :' the object of this double measure being the punishment of those who were implicated in the acquittal of Clodius, and the suppression of bribery at elections. Cf. *ep.* 18. 3 *facto senatus consulto de ambitu, de iudiciis: nulla lex perlata.* There is scarcely a doubt that this is the proper text and interpretation of the passage, for *habitarent* is the MS reading, while *cuius modi* would be a natural and easy corruption of the more unusual phrase *cuius domi.* In addition to this, the consul had been active in procuring the acquittal of Clodius. *Ut apud magistratus inquiri liceret* has been usually understood as follows: 'that it shall be allowable to search the houses of magistrates :' but the objection to this interpretation is twofold, (i) that it makes the two clauses almost identical, and (ii) that the measure in question is afterwards referred to thus: *ut de iis qui ob iudicandum pecuniam accepissent, quaereretur (ad Att.* I. 17. 8). For *adversus rempublicam* (*esse* or *facere*), cf. *ad Att.* II. 24. 3 *contra rempublicam esse facturum.* The other explanations are as follows:

(i) That *cuius modi* is to be taken as equivalent to *quoscunque:* 'that, if they harboured agents of whatever kind, it should be regarded as a State offence.'

(ii) To leave out *alterum,* on the ground that what follows is only a clause of the same decree: 'that a commission should be held before the magistrates to determine what sort of agents they held to be prejudicial to the State.'

But in this case there is no regular sequence to *unum,* while the words *in consulem facta* remain pointless and unexplained. Add to which *haberent adversus rempublicam* is, to say the least, a most questionable phrase.

Divisores] 'Bribery agents,' to be carefully distinguished from a class of the same name who were legally authorised to distribute certain funds among the tribes, and to whom reference is made in *Ep.* 18. 4 *tribulis enim tuus est, et Sextus pater eius numos vobis dividere solebat.* That largesses of this kind were occasionally supplied by the State itself is clear from the phrase *contionalis hirudo aerarii* in § 11.

§ 13 *Contra legem Aeliam*] An emendation which I have ventured to introduce into the text on my own authority, as the Medicean MS, on which we are mainly dependent for the text of the letters, is a comparatively late one, in which the contraction of *contra* into *contr.* or *coñ* might not unreasonably be expected to occur. *Qui magistratum simul cum lege Aelia iniit* is the usual reading, which has been rejected as hopeless by Ernesti, Schütz and Matthiae, all of whom omit the words *cum lege Aelia* from their text. Nor is it difficult to see that the fault, whatever it is, lies with the words *simul cum*, which, as they at present stand, are Latin for nothing—certainly not for *salva lege Aelia* (Gronov.), or for *tribunatum inivit servatis auspiciis ex lege Aelia* (Manut.), while their juxtaposition with the ablative *lege* is against our separating them thus: *qui, simul cum iniit magistratum lege Aelia, solutus est Aelia et Fufia.* Moreover it is scarcely possible that Lurco can have been elected to office otherwise than by a direct breach of the Aelian law, if we compare the sarcasm 'bono auspicio claudus' with the first clause of the law in question, *ut auspicato omnia fierent in comitiis.* As the next step, we may fairly assume that such a breach of the law would be alluded to by Cicero in a passage like the present, and I have therefore little hesitation in obtaining this sense by the slight alteration of *cum* into *coñ* (contra). By removing the word *cum*, the difficulty of separating *simul* from the ablatives which follow is removed with it, while a most forcible rendering is secured for the passage, 'Elected in defiance of the law and then formally released from its obligations.' In respect to the relative *qui*, we may either omit it as an interpolation consequent on the corruption of the rest of the sentence, or, if it is to be retained, supply the verb *est*, which I have introduced in brackets. In either case, *simul* will be equivalent to *simul cum*, a poetic usage which is not uncommon in Cicero.

[The above note was already in type when I received the following kind communication from Mr Munro, the late Professor of Latin: "The Medicean reading is *insimul cum*, not *simul cum*, of which the following is a simple and perhaps not unsatisfactory correction: *qui magistratum insimulatum lege Aelia iniit*, 'who entered upon a magistracy impeached by the Lex Aelia,' etc."]

Aelia et Fufia] The clauses of the *Lex Aelia* were three in number:

(i) Ut auspicato omnia fierent in comitiis.

(ii) Ut obnuntiatione facta dirimantur comitia.

(iii) Ut liberum esset intercedere, quibus intercedendi ius erat.

The single clause of the *Lex Fufia* ran thus:

Ne fastis diebus cum populo ageretur.

Casaubon enlarges upon the origin and import of these laws, the main object of which was to check the increasing power of the *plebs*. It was consequently with a bad precedent, though a good object, that they were relaxed for the purpose of passing a bribery law—a precedent which was afterwards pleaded by Clodius, Vatinius and others, when in later days they defied them and at last procured their abrogation. Cf. *pro Sest*. XV. 33, *post red. in Sen*. V. 11.

Comitia] i.e. for the election of the consuls. They were postponed to allow of the passing of the bribery law.

Claudus] *Malum auspicium erat quod legem claudus ferret* (Ern.), in illustration of which Mr Watson instances the apprehension which was felt at Sparta concerning the succession of Agesilaus (Plut. *Ages*. 3). By *bono auspicio* Cicero implies that no veto was put upon the measure, though, as a matter of fact, it never became law. Cf. *Ep*. 18. 3.

Novi est] 'The law in question contains the following novelty, that whoever promises a largess to the tribes without paying it shall be held excused, while, if he has once paid it, he shall be bound throughout his lifetime to pay 3000 sesterces per annum to each of the tribes. My remark was that Clodius had lived in the observance of this law, since he was for ever promising money and never paying it.'

Pronunciarit] 'Held out hopes of a largess' (cf. *or. pro Planc*. XVIII. 45, *pro Cluent*. XXIX. 78): a less decided word than *promittere*, and for that reason used in the present instance, where, as Casaubon remarks, *promittere* would imply a defiance of the law.

Si non dederit] Because, unless he had once paid it, there was no legal proof that the money had been promised. But there was probably another and more important reason in the fact that the sudden intermission of such a largess would have been liable to produce a serious disturbance among the lower classes.

ἀποθέωσιν] 'My consulship or deification (as Curio used to call it in days of yore) will, if this fellow be elected, sink to the level of a farce. So we must e'en take it stoically as you do, and not care a straw for the consulships we were so proud of.'

Curio] *dictitare solebat videri sibi eos, qui consulatum essent adepti, paene deos esse factos et diis pares.* Casaub.

Hic] Auli filius, i.e. Lucius Afranius.

Fabulam mimum] 'A play, that is a farce,' like ἴρηξ κίρκος and the phrases so common in Homer. This reading and interpretation, which is accepted by Matthiae and Schütz, is certainly preferable to most of the others which have been proposed in its place, e.g. *fama* (al. *fabula*) *imum*, 'will be nowhere in popular estimation;' or again, *famam mimum*, 'will be but a farcical reputation.' The possible alternative is *fabam mimum*, which is retained by some of the best editors, including Orelli, and is understood as a reference to the child's game noticed in Tac. *Ann.* XIII. 15, and Hor. *Ep.* I. 59 *at pueri ludentes, Rex eris, aiunt, Si recte facias*. As a parallel passage we may compare the following from Seneca (*de morte Claud.* cap. 9), *olim magna res erat Deum fieri: iam fama minimam fecit: etiam pessimi quique illam affectant*. *Fabam manium*, a conjecture which has arisen from the word ἀποθέωσις above, and which is approved of by Boot, seems to me intolerable.

Non flocci facteon] The phrase *flocci facere* appears again in *Ep. ad Att.* XIII. 50. 3.

§ 14] 'In reference to your statement that you have given up the idea of visiting Asia, I may say for myself that I would rather you had gone, for I am afraid it may cause you some inconvenience in a matter affecting your interests.' The words *ista re* may refer either to the disappointment and annoyance of Quintus at the abandonment of the proposed visit, or (2) to the loss which his administration would suffer from the absence of such a friend, or (3) to some private affairs which required the presence of Atticus in Asia. The last suggestion is the most probable from a comparison with *cuiusmodi istae res sint* (I. 14. 7), and other similar passages, especially as the change in question was made at the instance of Cicero, though, to judge from the next letter, he was reluctant to acknowledge the fact.

§ 15 *Epigrammatis*] The Greek ἐπιγράμμασιν. For the subject and character of these, cf. Corn. Nep. *Att.* 18, where they are described as inscriptions intended for insertion under the statues of certain distinguished Romans, which had been placed by Atticus in his Amaltheum in Epirus. The passage in question serves also to fix the meaning of the verb *ponere*, which otherwise might have been understood of literary composition, as in *ponere lucum artifices* (Pers. *sat.* I. 70). There is much vanity and little courtesy in Cicero's acknowledgment of the compliment.

Chilius] Cf. *Ep.* I. 9. 2, from which I should prefer to take *reliquerit* in its literal sense, 'has left me.' Matthiae, however, understands it to mean 'has neglected my praises.' For *Archias* and his poem in praise of Cicero's consulship cf. the argument of the *or. pro Archia*, delivered in the year 692.

Lucullis] i.e. in honour of Lucius and Marcus Lucullus on the subject of the Mithridatic war (*or. pro Arch.* IX. 21). 'And I am much afraid that, having completed his poem on the Luculli, he has now got his eye on a Caecilian drama.' By *Caecilianam* he means Q. Caecilius Metellus Numidicus and his son Pius, while in the word *fabulam* there is an allusion to the plays of the comic poet Caecilius.

§ 16 *Antonio*] In reference, no doubt, to his proposed visit to Asia, and to the letter of advice which Cicero had sent to Antonius on the subject of his Macedonian debts. Cf. *Ep.* I. 13. 1.

Manlio] Titus Manlius. He was engaged in business at Thespiae. Cf. *Ep. ad div.* XIII. 22. 1, but the reading itself varies between *Manlio* and *Mallio*.

Cui darem] 'Because I could not find a trustworthy messenger, and, what is more, wasn't sure of your address. However, I have paid you out now.'

Valde te vindicavi] 'I have taken my revenge,' i.e. for your reproaches on my laziness in *Ep.* 5. 3, 6. 1, and elsewhere. This allusion to the unusual length of the present letter is precisely what we should have expected, and how so admirable a reading can have been displaced in favour of *valde te venditavi*, 'I have been loud in your praise,' I am at a loss to imagine. The long passage which has intervened since the mention of Antonius is alone fatal to the introduction of *venditavi*. *Vale*, which appears in several editions instead of *valde*, is abrupt and out of place.

§ 18] 'I want you to write me word what your Amaltheum is like,—how decorated and how laid out: also to send me any poems or legends you have on the subject of Amalthea. I have a fancy for making one at Arpinum. I shall be sending you shortly some writings of mine, but at present have nothing in a finished state.'

NOTES.

In Arpinati] Cf. *Ep.* II. 1. 11, *Amalthea mea te exspectat et indiget tui.*

LETTER XVII.

Epitome of Contents] § 1—4 *The difference which had arisen between Quintus and Atticus.* § 5—7 *His own relations with Atticus.* § 8, 9 *The state of affairs at Rome, and the estrangement of the knights from the Senate.* § 10 *His own policy and his friendship with Pompeius.* § 11 *The forthcoming consular election, and the expected arrival of Atticus.*

§ 1 *Varietas voluntatis*] The precise cause of the dispute is unknown. We might have been led to ascribe it to the refusal of Atticus to accompany him to his province except for the words *post sortitionem provinciae* (§ 1), which shew that the grievance was one of longer standing, though it was clearly aggravated by the refusal in question (§ 7). Another natural supposition would have been that it arose out of the troubles which already existed between Quintus and his wife Pomponia. But here again we are met with the words *nam sic intelligo, ut nihil a domesticis vulneris factum sit, illud quidem, quod erat, eos certe sanare potuisse*: which imply that, though her conduct widened the breach between them, it was still not the primary cause of the quarrel.

Sauciumque esse eius animum] 'That his feelings had been wounded and his mind beset with fancies.' The word *esse* is omitted in the best MS, and might well be spared. On the other hand, to leave out *et* with Schütz and Nobbe, who read the sentence thus, *sauciumque eius animum insedisse quasdam odiosas suspiciones*, is to introduce a construction most unusual in Cicero.

§ 2 *Mollis*] 'susceptible.' Cf. *ad Att.* III. 9. 1, in which he uses the words *mollissimo animo* to describe the character of Quintus, 'a man of a very sensitive disposition.'

§ 3 *Non parcam tuis*] The sister of Atticus in particular, to whom he had already referred in the word *domesticis*.

§ 4 *Ecquid tantum causae sit*] 'Whether there is in them any adequate reason for your annoyance.'

Agilitatem] 'This vivacity, if I may use the term, and susceptibility of temperament, are as a rule indicative of goodness.' The above seems to me a far more natural arrangement of the words than to join *naturae plerumque bonitatis*, 'is usually of the nature of goodness,' as the passage is commonly interpreted.

§ 5] 'One part of your letter was quite uncalled for, wherein you detail the opportunities of advancement either at home or abroad, which you have allowed to escape you both on other occasions and during the time of my consulship. For I know full well the nobleness and greatness of your disposition, nor, to the best of my belief, has there ever been a discrepancy between us excepting as regards the choice of a profession, when a feeling of ambition led me to the pursuit of office, while you were induced by other and more praiseworthy motives to prefer an honourable repose. More by token in that true glory, which is the reward of integrity, energy and a strict adherence to principle, I regard you as standing higher than the rest of us, myself included, while in affectionate devotion to my interests, next to the affection of my brother and my family, the first place I give to you.'

Aliis temporibus] This and similar allusions make it evident that, in spite of the words *mallem ut ires* in the former letter, it was in obedience to the wishes of Cicero, expressed or unexpressed, that Atticus had declined the post.

Voluntatem institutae vitae] ἡ τοῦ βίου προαίρεσις.

Quum...discessi] 'second only to.' Cf. *Ep. ad div.* I. 9. 18, and again VI. 12. 2 *Caesaris familiares...quum ab illo discesserint me habent proximum.*

Primas tibi defero] sub. *partes.*

§ 6 *Sermonis communicatio*] 'That interchange of thought which used to be so pleasant between you and me.'

§ 7] The passage which follows destroys all the value of the foregoing as a natural expression of feeling: shewing as it does that it was merely an official statement necessitated by the request of Atticus, who wished that his motives, so scantily acknowledged by Cicero, should no longer be misconstrued by the world at large. This much at all events is plain from the context, and it does not reflect much credit on Cicero, that he was anxious to have Atticus near at hand in the troubles which he saw were approaching, and had accordingly discountenanced his visit to Asia, leaving Atticus the while to bear the brunt of Quintus' displeasure and the charge of inconsistency with the Roman public.

Verecundia] 'Has been repeatedly prevented by a natural bashfulness on both sides.'

Incommoditate] 'And in all the discomfort which has been caused you by the estrangement and irritation of his feelings there is yet this one advantage, that myself and your other friends have at last received evidence in your own handwriting of your reasons for declining the province, and shall believe in consequence that your refusal to accompany him was due to no want of harmony and agreement between you, but to a deliberate decision on the part of yourself alone. So the ties which have been broken will one day be made good, while our own, which have been so scrupulously guarded, will retain their sanctity as before.'

Discidio] *dissidio* al.; but cf. Madv. in *Exc.* II. *ad Cic. de fin.* p. 812.

§ 8] 'My lot here is cast in a weak, unhappy and unstable commonwealth. For you must have heard, I think, that my friends the knights have almost broken themselves off from the Senate, their first serious grievance being this, that a proposition was carried by a decree of the house for a commission of inquiry on those who had given a verdict for money.

'As ill-luck would have it, I was not present when the decree was passed, so, on finding that the displeasure of the equestrian order was great, though they did not give expression to it, I took the Senate to task with wonderful dignity, I flatter myself, and, considering the topic was rather a delicate one, my speech was very impressive and eloquent.

'Now listen to another caprice of the knights, well-nigh intolerable: however I not only tolerated it, but, what is more, made the best of it. The knights, who farmed the taxes of Asia on lease from the censors, laid a complaint before the house that, carried away by their eagerness, they had taken the contract at too high a rate: they requested accordingly that it might be cancelled. I was their leading counsel, or rather, I should say their junior: for it was Crassus who urged them to hazard the demand. The matter was calculated to excite jealousy, the request was discreditable and argued a want of consideration. There was the greatest danger that, if they obtained none of their demands, they would come to an open rupture with the Senate. In this matter too I was of the greatest assistance to them, and secured them a hearing before a crowded and conciliatory audience, while on the 1st and 2nd of December I made a long speech myself on the respect due to the orders and the advantages of harmony. Not that the matter is ended yet: but the consent of the Senate is secured, for Metellus the consul elect was the only speaker on the other side. Nay I am wrong: our hero Cato had intended to oppose it, but owing to the shortness of the day his turn did not come. So you see that, true to my purpose and principles, I am maintaining to the best of my power the harmony I have cemented. Yet in spite of all this (for you know I am trusting to a reed), I have paved a way, and a safe one too I hope, by which to retain my influence. I cannot tell you downright what it is in a letter: however I will throw you out a gentle hint of my meaning. I am on the best possible terms with Pompeius. I know what your comment will be. I will use caution where caution is necessary, and on a future occasion I will write to you at greater length about my plans for the government of the State.'

Ob iudicandum] i.e. in the Clodian trial. Boot raises an objection to this construction, and proposes to read *ob rem indicandam*. But there is really no analogy whatever between the phrase *ob dicendum* (for *ob ius dicendum*), which is rightly quoted as faulty in Quint. *inst. or.* V. 10. 87, and the one we are at present considering. The word *iudicare* is complete in itself, while in the other phrase *ius* is manifestly required to make the meaning intelligible. It is true however that in reverting to the subject in a later letter (II. 1. 8) Cicero uses the full phrase.

Pecuniam accepissent] The word *pecuniam* is not essential, and is omitted by Matthiae on the strength of a similar passage in the *or. pro Cluent.* 103.

In causa non verecunda] The gentlest of terms for a most disgraceful transaction, and, as the Senate was in this case on the side of justice, Cicero's conduct is the more inexcusable. In a subsequent letter (*Ep.* II. 1. 8) he condemns it himself in somewhat stronger terms: *quid verius quam in iudicium venire qui ob rem iudicandam pecuniam acceperit? censuit hoc Cato: adsensit senatus...quid impudentius publicanis renuntiantibus?* We are glad to find from the same passage that Cicero failed to carry his point.

§ 9 *Asiani*] *Asiae publicani.* Boot objects to the phrase (which is however the regular one) on the ground that *Asianus* can only mean a 'native of Asia.' Accordingly in Juv. *sat.* VII. 13, he explains *equites Asiani* as *servi ex Asia oriundi, qui manumissi ordini equestri adscripti sunt,* and in the present instance has even admitted into his text *Asiam qui de censoribus conduxerunt.*

Induceretur]= διαγράφειν, to obliterate the writing by drawing the thick end of the stilus across the wax.

Adeo] i.e. 'princeps *vel potius* secundus,' as Boot understands it, a sense of *adeo* which, though rare, is not unexampled in Cicero. In a former edition I had suggested the following rendering, as more in accordance with the usual force of the word: 'I was their senior and junior counsel in one, *senior* if you take into account the service I did them, *junior* if you regard the fact that I didn't originate the plea.'

Erat dicturus] Against the proposition, as we find from *Ep.* II. 1. 8, *restitit et pervicit Cato.* The indulgence they claimed was afterwards granted to them by Caesar during his consulship.

§ 10 *Conglutinatam concordiam*] Cf. *or. in Pis.* III. 7 : *ita est a me consulatus peractus...ut multitudinem cum principibus, equestrem ordinem cum senatu coniunxerim.*

§ 11 *Cum eo coire*] The best commentary on the text is the following passage from Suetonius (*Jul.* 19): *e duobus consulatus competitoribus, L. Lucceio M. que Bibulo, [Caesar] Lucceium sibi adiunxit: pactus ut is, quoniam inferior gratia esset pecuniaque polleret, numos de suo communi nomine per centurias pronunciaret. qua cognita re optimates, quos metus ceperat, nihil non ausurum eum in summo magistratu concordi ac consentiente collega, auctores Bibulo fuerunt tantumdem pollicendi: ac plerique pecunias contulerunt, ne Catone quidem abnuente eam largitionem e re publica fieri.*

Per Arrium] Cf. II. 5. 2: *de istis rebus exspecto tuas litteras: quid Arrius narret, quo animo se destitutum ferat,* and again II. 7. 2, *iam vero Arrius consulatum sibi ereptum fremit.*

Coniungi] i. e. *per coitionem.* This is better than to take the words *per C. Pisonem* as signifying that he would use the agency of Piso to settle the differences which are known to have existed between himself and Caesar. (Cf. *de bell. civ.* III.)

Modeste rogo] 'I ask you respectfully for what I desire above measure.' The reading *moleste* is less forcible, and moreover a very unusual phrase.

LETTER XVIII.

Epitome of Contents.] § 1 *His need of a friend in the absence of his brother and Atticus.* § 2 *His domestic troubles and the unhappy state of the republic since the Clodian verdict.* § 3 *The estrangement of the equites from the Senate and the prevailing anarchy.* § 4 *The proposed adoption of Publius Clodius into the plebeian order.* § 5 *The character of Metellus and Afranius.* § 6 *The Agrarian measure of Flavius. The policy of Pompeius, of Crassus, and* § 7 *of Cato.* § 8 *His eager anticipation of a visit from Atticus.*

§ 1 *Scito deesse*] This being a purely formal phrase (cf. *Ep.* III. 1) the word *scito* may be omitted in translation : 'I feel the want of nothing so much.' Of *eum* in the sense of *talem* we have already had repeated examples. Cf. *Ep.* 10. 6: *me autem eum et offendes erga te et audies,* etc. As regards the distinction between *quicum* and *quocum*, we may gather from a comparison of the passages in which they occur that *quocum* is the definite and *quicum* the more general word. For instance, in *Ep. ad div.* IV. 1. 1, XII. 18. 2, and *Lael.* VI. 22, where, as in the case before us, no particular object is specified, we find that *quicum* is the acknowledged reading.

Colloquar] *quum loquar* Klotz, a reading which gives a finish and completeness to the construction, but for that very reason detracts something from the ease and simplicity of the language.

ἀφελέστατος] 'most guileless, open-hearted of brothers.' It is used literally of a path which is smooth and unencumbered with stones (ἀ and φελλός), and the positive adverb occurs in *Ep. ad Att.* VI. 1. 8, *tu sceleste suspicaris, ego ἀφελῶς scripsi.* In *Ep.* II. 25. 1 he refers to the lines ἑλικτὰ κοὐδὲν ὑγιὲς ἀλλὰ πᾶν περὶξ Φρονοῦντες to denote the opposite character.

En tellus!] 'See what a world is mine!' I have adopted the reading of Matthiae, with the slight alteration of *me tellus!* into [*mei*] *en tellus!* which is required to make the passage translate.

Metellus non homo sed etc. is the more commonly received reading, but, in addition to the extravagance of the metaphor, exception has been taken to the introduction of Metellus, on the ground that his friendship with Cicero was not strong enough to justify the mention of him in such close connection with Quintus and Atticus. The latter argument cannot, I think, be pressed in the face of such passages as § 5 of the present letter and § 4 of the next; but the former objection has always appeared to me insuperable, more especially as the quotation from the *Philoctetes* of Accius is clearly no description of character, but rather of Cicero's own isolation in the world of politics. [Cf. Ov. *Her.* X. 18.] The following had occurred to me as a possible emendation: *et amantissimus mei Metellus. Non homo* etc., if we can suppose Metellus to have already left Rome for the suppression of the insurrection in Gaul. But it is perhaps safer to think that we may have lost the word or words which would have given to the quotation its connection with what precedes, and I have therefore preferred to print the sentence as above rather than to omit the words *me tellus* altogether, or to explain the quotation which follows as descriptive of the character of Quintus—a character with which they have nothing in common.

It remains to notice the ingenious but (I fear) too elaborate emendation of Schütz: *et amantissimus mei, et illius nunc domus est littus atque aër et solitudo mera.*

Mellito Cicerone] who was now four years old.

Ambitiosae] 'For those political and counterfeit friendships make a certain dash in the eyes of the world, but confer withal no home enjoyment.'

Tempore matutino] So Martial, *Ep.* IV. 8, *prima salutantes atque altera continet hora*, and *ad div.* IX. 20. 3.

Aures nactus tuas] 'Of which, methinks, if I could once get you to listen, I would unburden myself in the course of a single stroll.' For *ambulationis* cf. *Ep. ad. div.* II. 12. 2, *cum una mehercule ambulatiuncula atque uno sermone nostro omnes fructus provinciae non confero.*

§ 2 *Aculeos omnes et scrupulos*] 'The thorns and stones which beset the path of my family life I will hide from you, and indeed I do not care to entrust a letter on such subjects to a stranger. Not that they are so *very* painful—for I would not have you alarm yourself—but still they rankle and oppress me, and I have no loving friend to lay them by his counsel and advice.' He can scarcely be alluding, as some have supposed, to the disagreements between himself and Terentia, which finally ended in her divorce: for, if this were so, the previous sentence, *tantum requietis habeam quantum cum uxore consumitur*, would be worse than a common-place.

Et voluntas etiam] I have adopted the very ingenious emendation of Schütz, with the addition of the word *etiam* which he omits. This is a closer adherence to the MSS than the equally ingenious suggestion of Orelli, *tamen eam iam ipsa medicina deficit*, 'though I am with it heart and soul it is now past all cure.' Either of the above readings, even if it does not represent the precise words of Cicero, has at any rate a better right to stand in place of them than the unintelligible sentence which Nobbe and the other editors sanction, apparently without a doubt of its authenticity. It is just possible however that the passage might be made translatable by reading *voluntate* instead of *voluntas*, 'notwithstanding by deliberate choice it (sc. *respublica*) declines the needful remedy.' This suggests itself to me as a less violent alteration than to reject *voluntas* altogether (with Boot and others) as a gloss on *animus*, who read the sentence thus: *in republica vero, quamquam animus est praesens, tamen etiam atque etiam ipsa medicinam refugit.*

Fabulae Clodianae] 'The case of the Clodian scandal.' By understanding *fabula* in this sense rather than that of a 'stage-play' we can explain *causam* in its usual legal signification, and at the same time avoid the confusion of metaphors upon which Orelli comments thus: *exspectabas potius scenam*.

§ 3 *Adflicta*] 'The republic has received its death-blow, thanks to a venal and debauched tribunal. Now observe the consequences!'

Suspiritu] *Suspiratu* al., but, though found in Ovid (*Met.* XIV. 129), the form is apparently not Ciceronian.

De ambitu] Cf. I. 16. 13.

De iudiciis] Cf. I. 17. 8. It is scarcely consistent or honest of Cicero to complain that these measures had not become law, when he had himself opposed them might and main, as he tells us in the previous letter (*in causa non verecunda admodum gravis et copiosus fui*).

Exagitatus] 'The Senate is angry and the knights are estranged from it. Thus has this year (693) beheld the overthrow of two pillars of the State, which my exertions had set up; the Senate has lost its dignity, and the harmony of the two orders is destroyed.' Meriv. The importance of this passage cannot be over-estimated in forming a judgment of Cicero's character. It records the death-blow of the coalition for which he had been scheming, and from this point in consequence his hopes were more than ever centred in himself.

Instat hic nunc [*ille*] *annus*] 'We have now upon us a memorable year.' It is surprising to find that no editor has suggested the omission of the word *ille*, the presence of which in the MSS is so easily accounted for by the corresponding passage three lines above. The adjective *egregius* is against our taking it as equivalent to *talis*, which is the only available sense if it is to be retained in its present position.

Sacra iuventatis] *Iuventatis aedem vovit M. Livius Salinator a.* 547, *locavit idem censor a.* 550, *dedicavit C. Licinius Lucullus a.* 563, *et tunc primum ludi facti sunt.* Boot. Memmius—so well-known in connection with the poems of Lucretius and Catullus—was curule aedile at the time, and therefore under other circumstances would have presided at the ceremonies.

Ille pastor] 'The legendary Paris.'

Agamemnonem] Lucius Lucullus, the brother of the former. He had conducted the campaign against Mithridates. The allusion in the text is obscure, and three suggestions have been made to explain it: (i) that he had been the prosecutor in a charge against L. Lucullus; (ii) that in his capacity of tribunus plebis he had refused to sanction his triumph on his return from the East; or (iii) 'quia eius uxorem pariter stupravit.' Ern.

§ 4 *Numos vobis dividere*] On the subject of these *divisores* cf. note on *Ep.* I. 16. 12. I prefer to understand it of an authorised largess rather than of an illegal distribution in which Atticus had been interested.

Traducit] 'Wants to transfer.' This process of adoption was called *adrogatio*, and the object of it was to qualify Clodius for the tribunate and enable him in this capacity to oppose the measures of Cicero. It should by rights have taken place before the *comitia curiata*, and the proposal to bring it instead before the *comitia tributa*, or general assembly of the people, was no doubt the result of a secret arrangement between Clodius and Herennius. The person into whose family Clodius was nominally adopted is mentioned in cap. 13 of the *or. pro dom.* as one Fonteius. The adoption was favoured by Caesar, and indeed carried at last by his agency. (Cf. Suet. *Iul.* 20.) For an account of the whole transaction and its influence on the future of Cicero, cf. Merivale, p. 106 ff.

Accepi] 'I gave him my customary welcome in the senate, but never saw anything more stolid than the fellow.' For this use of *accipere*, cf. *Tusc.* IV. 36. 78, *quo te modo accepissem, nisi iratus essem.*

§ 5] 'Metellus is a grand consul and quite devoted to your humble servant: but he has impaired his influence by regarding the bill in question as purely a matter of form. As for the son of Aulus—great heavens!—what a dastardly and spiritless soldier it is! how deservedly he has met his fate, which is to lend his ears to the abuse of Palicanus. We have from Flavius the scheme of an Agrarian law, ill-considered in its details and nearly identical with the Plotian. But all this while there is no statesman, no nor the ghost of one among us. Pompeius my friend—for such he is and I wish you to know it—who had in him the making of one, now maintains in silence the dignity of his triumphal robe. From Crassus never a word to give offence. What the rest are you know by this time—such fools that they think they can sacrifice the State and yet save their fishponds. One man, and but one, there is to protect the republic, and that rather by his firmness and honesty than by any talent or tact: Cato I mean, who for the last two months has been keeping those wretched taxgatherers, once his devoted admirers, on the rack of expectation, and will not allow them to get an answer from the Senate. In consequence we are compelled to postpone all measures till a reply has been given to them, and so I suppose even the reception of the deputies will be put off for the present. You see by this how trouble-tost I am, and, if from what I say you can supply what I suppress, come and see me at last, and, although I may not be inviting you to pleasant quarters, shew notwithstanding that you prize my affection so highly as to wish to enjoy it even at the cost of these discomforts. For to prevent your being registered by proxy I will have a special notice made and posted up throughout the town. Remember also that to return your name amongst the last is too highly suggestive of the shop!'

Dicis causa] = ὁσίας ἕνεκα, 'for appearance sake,' (cf. Plin. 28. 2), *dicis* being in all probability connected with the Greek δίκη, which is common enough in the Latinized form of *dica*, e.g. *sexcentas scribito iam mihi dicas, nil do* (Ter. *Phorm.* IV. 3. 63).

Habet...promulg.] Notwithstanding Orelli's able vindication of the text, the passage, both as regards the Latinity and the interpretation, is still far from satisfactory. The most obvious objection to the received explanation is that it requires a stronger word than *habet* (νομίζει) to make it effective, even if we understand the verb *habere* in the stronger and less usual sense of 'recognises,' 'entertains.' This difficulty however might be easily surmounted by reading *perhibet* for *habet*. But the emphatic position of *habet* seems to shew that it represents a stronger idea than the one suggested, and I should myself prefer to translate *promulgatum habet* as = *promulgavit*, 'by formally proposing the bill in question about Clodius.' However we may explain the passage, it is at all events clear that any countenance Metellus may have given to the bill was given under a misunderstanding of its aim and object, for, when convinced of its real character, he opposed it in every possible way, and, when Clodius at a later date was a candidate for the tribunate, he objected to him on the ground that his adoption had been illegal. I have reserved for final notice an emendation of the passage which is accepted by Schütz: *quod habere dicit causam promulgatum illud idem de Clodio*, the objections to which are (1) the order of the words, and (2) the use of *promulgatum* as a substantive, of which I can find no other example in Cicero. In addition to which I can discover no adequate grounds for his rejection of the phrase *dicis causa*, which is, on the contrary, a favourite one with our author. Cf. *Verr. II.* IV. 24, and *or. pro. Mur.* 12.

Illud quidem] *Illud idem* vulg., a reading with which I have long been dissatisfied, and of which, as I venture to think, the alteration of *idem* into *quidem* is an easy and effective correction.

Miles] The word is peculiarly suitable to *Afranius*, who, as I have already noticed, had been one of the lieutenants of Pompeius in Asia. It is strange that, not content with *miles*, Muretus should have proposed so weak a word as *millies* in its place.

Palicano] M. Lollius Palicanus (cf. I. 1. 1), a tribune of the people, of such infamous character that, when he was a candidate for the consulship in A. U. C. 687, the consul Piso declared that, in case of his election, he should decline to return him (Val. Max. III. 8. 3).

Os...praebeat] Cf. Liv. IV. 35, *praebere ad contumeliam os*, and Tac. *hist*. III. 3. 1, *praeberi ora contumeliis*.

§ 6 *Agraria*] This proposition, which had for its object the partition of lands among the soldiers of Pompeius, never became law. Cf. Dio Cass. XXXVII. p. 52.

Plotia] The date and particulars of this measure are unknown. Like the present, it was clearly a tribunician scheme.

Togulam illam pictam] Notice the disparaging diminutive. The full details of his triumphal entry are given in Vell. Pat. II. 40; and Dio Cass. XXXVII. 21.

Caeteros] In particular Lucullus, Q. Hortensius and L. Philippus. Cf. *hos piscinarios, Ep.* 19. 6, and II. 1. 7, *nostri autem principes digito se caelum putant attingere, si mulli barbati in piscinis sint qui ad manum accedant*.

§ 7 *Legationes*] See the note on *Ep.* 14. 5, and cf. *Ep. ad div.* I. 4. 1. The tactics of Cato on this occasion are alluded to as follows in the *or. pro Planc*. XIV. 34, *quum senatus impediretur quominus, id quod hostibus semper erat tributum, responsum equitibus Romanis redderetur*.

§ 8 *Quae scripsimus (tanta)*] It is of course impossible that the word *tanta* can retain its present position, although Boot justifies it as an attraction: while Matthiae now rejects as an interpolation the parenthesis *tanta es perspicacitate*, which appears in most of the editions. In place of *tanta* he proposes *cuncta*: but the omission of the former word is really all that is required, which may possibly have crept into its present place from the juxtaposition in some MS of the word *tanti* which occurs below.

Ne absens censeare] We find from Gellius that, in a speech delivered by P. Scipio Africanus during his censorship in the year 612, he condemns the practice as irregular and contrary to precedent. At the present time, however, the custom had become habitual, though the question remains open whether the names of absentees were given in through the provincial magistrate or collected (as Bekker maintains) by a special agent (*procurator*).

Sub lustrum] i.e. 'at the close of the proceedings.' Cf. Liv. I. 44, *Servius Tullius, censu perfecto...instructum exercitum omnem suovetauribus lustravit: idque conditum lustrum appellatum, quia is censendo finis factus est.*

Germani negociatoris] has been usually understood as a complimentary term for a 'true man of business,' a sense which the words will undoubtedly bear. But from the passage which follows, it is clear that Cicero wishes to hasten his friend's arrival, rather than to suggest a particular time for his coming, and it is therefore far more forcible to take the words *germani negociatoris* in the disparaging sense in which I see they are understood by Manutius, Schütz and Matthiae. The allusion is, in all probability, to the preoccupations of a man of business: though there is much to be said in favour of the more elaborate explanation suggested by Bekker: *negociatores, ne plus minusve quam haberent in censu profiterentur, quod aut rei suae aut fidei noceret, sub lustrum demum censorem adibant. atqui turpe erat Attico, equiti Romano, negociatoris morem sequi.*

LETTER XIX.

Epitome of Contents] § 1 *His own occupations.* § 2 *The disturbances in Gaul and the measures taken to repress them.* § 3 *The compliments paid by the Senate to Pompeius and himself.* § 4 *The Agrarian measure of Flavius.* § 5 *The schemes of Clodius.* § 6 *His own policy.* § 7 *His relations with Pompeius, and* § 8 *with the different parties in the State.* § 9 *The decree concerning Sicyon.* § 10 *The account of his consulship in Latin and Greek.* § 11 *The relations between Quintus and Atticus, and conclusion.*

§ 1 *Crebrior*] Cf. or. pro Planc. XXXIV. 83, *hoc frequenter in me congessisti saneque in eo creber fuisti.*

Absque argumento ac sent.] 'without a plot and purpose.' I have adopted the reading of Schütz, as it is quite impossible to believe that Cicero wrote either *nullam a me sino epistolam ad te sine argumento pervenire* as Boot edits the passage, or *nullam a me epistolam ad te sino sine argumento pervenire* as it appears in the edition of Matthiae: while the phrase *absque sententia*, which the former quotes from Quintilian (*inst. or.* VII. 2. 44), is in itself a sufficient justification of the text.

Amanti patriam] 'a patriotic citizen like yourself.'

§ 2 *Gallici belli versatur metus*] *Gallici versantur metus* (as Boot reads from a single MS), or *Gallici versantur motus*, are both of them preferable in form to the reading of the text: but the former is too bold to be admitted except on the strength of a parallel passage, while the addition of the words *in republica* are against our accepting the latter.

Fratres nostri] The Aedui in return for their services had received this title as a compliment from the Senate. Cf. Caes. *de bell. Gall.* I. 31, and *Ep. ad div.* VII. 10. 3.

Sequani permale pugnarunt] 'have made very bad hands at fighting.' But the word *Sequani* is probably an interpolation, while *Helvetii* on the other hand, which is omitted in the MSS, has been supplied from the context. Indeed the passage as a whole is indubitably corrupt, nor is it to be remedied by the emendation devised by Boot: *pugnam nuper malam pugnarunt*.

Provinciam] i.e. Gallia Narbonensis (cf. Caes. *de bell. Gall.* I. 7).

Sortirentur] 'that the two Gauls should be reserved for the consuls, troops levied, furloughs recalled, and ambassadors sent with full powers to treat with the states of Gaul, and to prevent, if possible, their coalition with the Helvetii. The ambassadors chosen are Metellus and Flaccus, and—to spoil the porridge—Lentulus.'

Vacationes ne valerent] This distinguishes the occasion in question from an ordinary *tumultus*, when such exemptions were not recalled (cf. *Phil.* VIII. 3).

Legati] Embassies with full powers consisted usually of three individuals—one of consular, one of praetorian, and the third of senatorial rank.

τὸ ἐπὶ τῇ φακῇ μύρον] A proverb used to denote fruitless labour—a costly sauce over a poor material. For the pun on the word *lens* (φακῇ) compare the well-known *guttam adspergit huic Bulbo* in the Cluentian speech.

Lentulus] Cn. Cornelius Lentulus is meant, who was consul in the year 681.

§ 3 *Mea sors*] In reference to the choice of the deputies, which was made either by lot, as on the present occasion, or else by suffrage (Tac. *Hist.* IV.).

ἐπιφωνήματα] 'For why should I court the praises of foreigners, when they grow in such plenty at home?'

§ 4] 'Our home affairs are in this condition. The Agrarian scheme of Flavius is being eagerly pressed at the instigation of Pompeius; but it has nothing in it to recommend it except its patron. From this measure, in obedience to the wishes of the meeting, I proceeded to remove all the clauses which infringed on private interests: for instance, I released from its operation all the land which had been State property so far back as the consulship of Mucius and Calpurnius: I ratified the ownership of the Sullan occupants: re-established the title of those persons at Volaterrae and Arretium, whose lands Sulla had confiscated but retained in his hands. One scheme only I did not reject, which had for its object the purchase of lands with the foreign revenue which should accrue in the next five years from the new imposts. To the whole of this Agrarian measure the Senate is mightily opposed in the belief that the aim of its promoters is the extension of the power of Pompeius. He on his part has applied himself in good earnest to the task of passing the law. My share in the matter was to secure the interests of private landholders, by which I won the heartfelt gratitude of the proprietors (for as you know I draw my followers from that well-to-do class), while at the same time I satisfied Pompeius and the people, as it was my wish to do, by the proposed purchase-scheme, in the careful ordering of which I saw a plan for draining the city of its scum, and for colonizing the waste lands of Italy.'

Agraria lex] The same as that mentioned in § 6 of the former letter. It had for its object the distribution of land among the soldiers of Pompeius. The *auctor legis* was usually some person of rank and influence, who undertook to recommend it to the people.

Habebat] *habet* Schütz, on the ground that the epistolary tense is only used of conditions which may be altered during the transmission of the letter.

P. Mucio L. Calpurnio consulibus] A. U. C. 621.

Volaterr. et Arret.] Their claims were advocated by Cicero in the speeches against Rullus, and sanctioned by Caesar during his first consulship in the year 695. (Cf. *Ep. ad. div.* XIII. 4. 4.)

Novis vectigalibus] He alludes to the new sources of revenue which had been opened up by the victories of Pompeius in the East. The subject supplies him with a constant fund of jokes, e.g. II. 16. 2, *nunc vero, Sampsicerame, quid dices? vectigal te nobis in monte Antilibano constituisse, agri Campani abstulisse.*

Agrariorum] Certainly not equivalent to *agripetarum*,

the party who from interested motives were in favour of the Agrarian law, and to whose claims as a rule Cicero was altogether opposed. On the contrary, they are alluded to in the sentence which follows: *populo autem et Pompeio satisfaciebam:* while the use of the word *confirmabam* in the earlier part of the narrative shews that by *agrariorum* he means the present wealthy proprietors, whose landed interests made them strong opponents of any revolutionary scheme.

Sentinam urbis exh.] The Greek ἄντλον εἴργειν. Boot illustrates the expression by a precisely similar passage in the *or. contr. Rull.* II. 26. 70, where, in answer to the remark of Rullus, *urbanam plebem nimium in republica posse, exhauriendam esse,* Cicero replies: *hoc enim verbo est usus, quasi de aliqua sentina...loqueretur.*

Bello] The disturbance in Gaul of which he has spoken above.

Ille alter] 'Afranius is such a fool that he doesn't even know the value of his purchase,' i.e. the consulship. Cf. *Ep.* 26. 12. In Ter. *Eun.* IV. 4. 23 we find the same phrase, *eo rediges me, ut, quid emerim, nesciam.*

§ 5 *Nequam atque egentem*] 'A mean and beggarly fellow.' The expression is used again of Hilarus in I. 12. 2.

§ 6 *Nonarum illarum Dec.*] Cf. *or. pro Flac.* XL. 102. *O nonae illae Decemb. quae me consule fuistis! quem ego diem vere natalem huius urbis aut certe salutarem appellare possum.*

Beatos] 'Rich,' 'well-to-do,' as in *Ep.* I. 14. 1 *beatis non grata.*

For *piscinarios* see the note on § 6 of the previous letter.

§ 7 *Adiudicarit*] One of these occasions is referred to by Cicero in the *de off.* I. 22. 78 *mihi quidem certe vir abundans bellicis laudibus Cn. Pompeius multis audientibus hoc tribuit, ut diceret frustra se triumphum tertium deportaturum fuisse, nisi meo in rempublicam beneficio, ubi triumpharet, esset habiturus.*

Illae res] 'The exploits in question were not done in a corner so as to need evidence, nor were they so questionable as to require praise.'

§ 8 *Inventutis*] Clodius and his friends. His bearing towards Clodius on this and another occasion (*Ep.* II. 1. 5 *itaque iam familiariter cum ipso cavillor ac iocor*) is thus noticed by Abeken: 'He behaved with more deference than was consistent with his own convictions towards Crassus,

Antonius, and at one time even towards Clodius.' (Meriv. p. 60.)

Asperum] 'In a word I have indulged in no severities, but yet in no lax measures to curry favour. On the contrary, my whole policy is so ordered that I shew myself firm in the interests of the State, while in my private relations I am compelled by the weakness of the good, the malice of the ill-disposed, and the hatred of the vicious to use a certain care and caution; and, while I form these new ties, I allow the crafty Sicilian of yore to whisper in my ears ever his old refrain: *Be wary and mistrustful: the sinews of the soul are these.*

Ita tamen] A condensed expression for *atque, licet illa faciam, ita tamen facio ut* etc.

Siculus] Epicharmus, though born at Cos, passed the greater portion of his life in Sicily. In the *Tusc. disp.* I. 8. 15 he is spoken of as *acutus nec insulsus homo ut Siculus*. In the present passage Schütz, Matthiae and the best editors omit the proper name as the addition of a later hand.

Cantilenam] Cf. *cantilenam eandem eam*, 'ever the same old song' (Ter. *Phorm.* III. 2. 10). This verse from Epicharmus is also referred to by Quintus Cicero in his pamphlet *de pet. cons.* cap. 10 *sobrius esto, atque* Ἐπιχάρμειον *illud teneto, nervos atque artus esse sapientiae non temere credere.*

§ 9] 'You are for ever writing to me about that matter of yours, for which I cannot now suggest a remedy. For the decree in question was passed with the entire consent of the more demonstrative members, though none of our party gave it their sanction. When you complain that I witnessed the draft of the bill, you might by referring to it have gathered that it was a different matter that was then before the house, and that the clause in question was an uncalled-for addition, for which the younger Servilius is to blame, who voted last; but no amendment can now be made. More by token the indignation meetings, which at the outset were thronged, have for a long time been discontinued. If, in spite of it, your blandishments can succeed in squeezing anything out of the Sicyonians, I should like you to let me know. I send you an account of my consulship in Greek. If you find anything in it which strikes one of your name and family as wanting in Greek scholarship, I wont make the excuse which Lucullus made to you, if I remember right, at Panhormus in the case of his history—that he had introduced a few barbarisms and solecisms at intervals to prove more conclusively that the whole was the work of a Roman. Anything of the kind that may appear in my treatise will be an unintentional slip. The

Latin version—that is, if I ever complete it—shall be forwarded to you. You may look out for a third in verse, that I may omit no possible means of self-laudation. Now don't say, *Your trumpeter's not dead:* for, if there is anything in the history of the world that more deserves my praise, all praise to it: all blame to me for not praising it in preference. Though, look you, what I write is no mere panegyric, but sober matter of fact. My brother Quintus is at pains to clear himself by a letter, and assures me that he has never spoken disparagingly of you to anyone. But we must sift the matter when we meet with all possible pains and care: only do come and see me at last. Our friend Cossinius who takes this letter appears to me to be a capital fellow, and a steady one to boot. Add to which he believes in you firmly, and is, in a word, precisely what your letter gave me to understand.'

§ 9 *De tuo autem negocio*] The decree relative to Sicyon, on the subject of which cf. *Ep.* 13. 1 and the note on the passage. The special object of the decree in question is nowhere mentioned by Cicero. Ernesti considers that it was simply a refusal on the part of the Senate to interfere between an individual and the members of a free state—an explanation which is certainly in accordance with the words which follow: *tu si tuis blanditiis tamen a Sicyoniis numulorum aliquid expresseris, velim me facias certiorem.* On the other hand, Schütz and Matthiae are of opinion that the object of the decree was to exempt the Sicyonians, in part at any rate, from the burden of taxation. A careful consideration of the passages in which the subject is mentioned, more especially of § 4 of the ensuing letter, has induced me to accept the latter as in all probability the correct view.

Summa pedariorum voluntate] For *summa* Ernesti suggests *sola*, but his objections to the received reading are scarcely satisfactory. In the *Journal of Philology* (New Series, vol. IV. no. 7, p. 113) will be found an admirable article by Mr D. B. Munro on the subject of the *pedarii*, in which he conclusively refutes the theory that they could *vote* but not *speak* in the assembly. The *discessio* (he says) was no equivalent to the modern division, but (as in *Ep. ad Att.* I. 20. 4) an incident in the middle of the debate, which was no more a legal vote than the cries of 'Agreed' in the English House of Commons, though the practical effect might be the same in both cases. It was in fact, or might be made, a running division, spread over the whole debate, and sensitive to every turn in the scale of opinion: adopted usually perhaps by the *pedarii*, i.e. senators who were too far down in the list to have an opportunity of speaking, *but also by senators who had already spoken.* He notices that in Liv. XXXVII. 34 these two ways of giving a silent vote are mentioned as alternatives: *aut verbo assentire aut pedibus in sententiam ire.*

Nostrum] i.e. senators who had held curule magistracies. These were ranked in the following order: *censorii, consulares, praetorii, aedilicii, tribunicii, quaestorii,* after which came those who had held no magistracy. The *princeps senatus* was as a rule the eldest person who had held the censorship.

Auctoritate] In the same way *praescriptio, auctoritates praescriptae* are the signatures by which the leading senators attested the draught of a decree. Cf. *ad div.* VIII. 8. 5. The phrase *esse ad scribendum* appears again in *Ep. ad div.* XII. 29. 2 *consulibus illis nunquam fuit ad scribendum.*

P. Servilio filio] who on this and similar occasions followed the lead of Cato. Cf. II. 1. 10 *quod Sicyonii te laedunt, Catoni et eius aemulatori attribuis Servilio.* The word *filius* is added to distinguish him from his father P. Servilius Isauricus, who was still living.

Conventus] These were not necessarily confined to senators, as Schütz and Matthiae have imagined, but were irregular meetings held by the interested parties outside the walls of the Senate-house.

§ 10 *Homini Attico*] Cf. ἀττικώτερα (*Ep.* 13. 5) and *puto te Latinis meis delectari, huic autem Graeco Graecum invidere* (*Ep.* 20. 6).

De suis historiis] On the subject of the Marsian campaign (Plut. *Luc.* cap. 1.). The word σόλοικα is equivalent to *barbara*, and is referred to the corrupt dialect of the Athenian colonists who settled at Soli in Cilicia.

τίς πατέρ' αἰνήσει;] The proverb is given in full by Plutarch in his *Life of Aratus*, ch. X. τίς πατέρ' αἰνήσει εἰ μὴ κακοδαίμονες υἱοί; and he appends the following comment: τοὺς ἀφ' αὑτῶν οὐδενὸς ἀξίους ὄντας, ὑποδυομένους δὲ προγόνων τινῶν ἀρεταῖς καὶ πλεονάζοντας ἐν τοῖς ἐκείνων ἐπαίνοις ὑπὸ τῆς παροιμίας ἐπιστομίζεσθαι. There is some difficulty, however, in determining its application in the present instance. It may mean: 'If praise of near relations is to be discouraged, much more by consequence the praise of self'—an explanation which suits the context well, and for which we have a near equivalent in English. Ernesti, on the other hand, would explain it thus: 'To praise your past life is, by comparison, to disparage your present.'

§ 11 *Cossinius*] Lucius Cossinius (*Ep.* 20. 6, II. 1. 1). He is mentioned again in *Ep. ad div.* XIII. 23. 1.

LETTER XX.

Epitome of Contents] § 1 *On the subject of their correspondence and the relations between Quintus and Atticus.* § 2 *His own position in the State and a justification of his friendship with Pompeius.* § 3 *His present and future policy.* § 4 *The decree relating to Sicyon.* § 5 *His opinion of the consuls.* § 6 *His literary work.* § 7 *The addition made to his library by the kindness of Paetus. A request to Atticus to hasten the time of his visit.*

§ 1 *e Pompeiano*] The neighbourhood of Pompeii was rich in villas. Thus, in addition to the one owned by Cicero, mention is made in the letters of one which had belonged to Marius (*ad div.* VII. 3), and another in the occupation of Pansa (*ad Att.* V. 3. 1).

Iudicium] Cf. *Ep.* 17. 5 *mihi enim perspecta est ingenuitas et magnitudo animi tui.*

A nobis atque nostris] Schütz is inclined to regard the words *nobis atque* as an interpolation, on the ground that in no other passage does Cicero impute blame to himself for the disagreement which had arisen between his brother and Atticus. But throughout the earlier portion of the 17th letter his tone, if not actually self-accusing, is still so strongly apologetic that we can easily see he was not altogether satisfied with his own part in the matter.

Moderatissimum fuisse] 'That you have shewn such forbearance.'

§ 2] 'Of the commonwealth you take a far-sighted and patriotic view, and your ideas are in harmony with my own: for I must not abandon my dignified position, nor yet trust myself unprotected within the enemy's camp: while the friend you mention is destitute alike of honour and dignity, mean and time-serving in everything.'

Intra alterius praesidia] Schütz compares the following passage in a subsequent letter: *neque enim eos solos arbitrabamur capi, qui in armatorum manus incidissent, sed eos nihilo minus, qui regionibus exclusi intra praesidia atque intra arma aliena venissent.*

Nihil amplum, nihil excelsum] This criticism of Pompeius is almost identical with that contained in an earlier letter (*Ep.* 13. 4).

Ad tranquillitatem meorum temp.] 'To ensure my peace of life.' That this was in reality his chief motive for forming the alliance may, in addition to other passages, be inferred from *Ep.* 9 of the following book: *si vero, quae de me pacta sunt, ea non servantur, in coelo sum ut sciat hic noster Hierosolymarius traductor ad plebem quam bonam meis putissimis orationibus gratiam retulerit, quarum exspecta divinam παλινῳδίαν.*

Cum aliqua levitate] 'Now if my conduct in this respect had involved a sacrifice of principle, no object in my idea would have been worth the cost. As it is, I have so managed matters throughout that I have lost no caste by being found in harmony with him, while he has gained much by his recognition of me. For the rest, I have laid my plans for the present and the future so as not to risk the imputation that my past achievements were the result of chance.'

The allusion in *probans* may be illustrated by a passage in *Ep.* 14. 2 *mihique, ut adsedit,* [Pompeius] *dixit se putare satis ab se etiam de istis* (al. *istius*) *rebus esse responsum.*

§ 3 *Meos bonos viros*] i.e. the *optimates,* as in *Ep.* 13. 3 and elsewhere.

It has been less correctly explained of the wealthy landowners who are mentioned in *Ep.* 19. 4 as *is noster exercitus, hominum, ut tute scis, locupletium,* but the words *hanc iram optimatum* which follow are conclusive in favour of the former view.

Σπάρταν] ἔλαχες, ταύταν κόσμει (IV. 6. 2), proverbial of one who has entered on a great inheritance which it becomes him to administer with credit.

Post Catuli mortem] His character is thus described in the *or. pro Sestio* (cap. 47): *quem neque periculi tempestas neque honoris aura potuit unquam de suo cursu vitae aut spe aut metu dimovere.*

Rhinton] A poet of Tarentum, who cultivated a species of burlesque tragedy.

Piscinarii nostri] Cf. I. 18. 8. 'The jealousy with which I am regarded by our friends the fish-ponders I will either describe to you in a future letter or reserve till our next meeting. From my place in the Senate nothing shall ever tear me, either because it is my duty, or my interest, or because I am by no means indifferent to the esteem of that assembly. In your dealings with Sicyon, as I have already hinted, you have not much to look for from the Senate. For there is no one at present to make a formal complaint. So, if you wait for that, you will have to wait. Fight your battle by some other means, if any are forthcoming. At the time when the decree was passed, too little heed was given to the interests involved, and a rush was made by the body of the house in favour of the motion. The time has not yet come for cancelling the decree, for, as I say, there are none to make a formal complaint, while it satisfies the malice of some, the sense of justice in others. Your friend Metellus makes a glorious consul. I have only one fault to find with him, that he is not sufficiently delighted at the news of peace in Gaul. He had, I suppose, set his heart on a triumph. Given moderation on this one point, all else in him is perfect. Afranius, on the contrary, plays so poor a part, that his consulship is no consulship at all but a stain on the reputation of our Great Pompeius.'

§ 4 *Iam*] 'Any longer' is the translation accepted by Schütz, who refers it to the discontinuance of the indignation meetings mentioned in § 9 of the previous letter. But surely the succeeding comments, *quare, si id exspectas, longum est*, and, more especially, *inducendi senatus consulti maturitas nondum est*, are decisive in favour of the rendering 'at present: as yet.'

Pedarii] Cf. § 9 of the last letter, and for *inducendi* cf. I. 17. 9 *ut induceretur locatio postulaverunt*.

§ 5 *Magni nostri ὑπώπιον*] Cf. I. 16. 12. This same Afranius is mentioned by Dio Cassius (XXXVII. 49) as a good dancer but a bad statesman. He was defeated by Caesar in the civil war in Spain ⸱ U.C. 705. For the word ὑπώπιον, a 'bruise on the face,' compare the well-known use of the verb ὑπωπιάζειν in the New Testament (*Ep. ad Corinth.* I. 9. 27).

§ 6 *Eum librum*] 'The copy in question.' For *retardantur* cf. II. I. 2 *quamquam ad me rescripsit iam Rhodo Posidonius, se, nostrum illud ὑπόμνημα quum legeret, quod ego ad eum ut ornatius de iisdem rebus scriberet miseram, non modo non excitatum esse ad scribendum, sed etiam plane perterritum. Quid quaeris? conturbavi Graecam nationem.*

§ 7 *L. Papirius Paetus*] An Epicurean, to whom many of the letters are addressed, e.g. *ad div.* IX. 16. His brother, Servius Claudius, had died in Greece, probably in Epirus, where he had left the books in question.

Per legem Cinciam] *Legem Cinciam flagitant, qua cavetur antiquitus ne quis ob causam orandam pecuniam donumve accipiat* (Tac. *Ann.* XI. 5). It was proposed by the tribune M. Cincius Alimentus, and passed in the consulship of Cornelius Cethegus and Sempronius Tuditanus, A. U. C. 550. 'As your friend Cincius tells me I may accept them notwithstanding the law which rejoices in his name, I said I would gladly do so if he would arrange for their conveyance. Now, as you love me and as you know I love you, set your friends, your clients, your guests, and even your freedmen and slaves to work to see that no scrap of them be lost.'

INDEX OF WORDS

TRANSLATED OR EXPLAINED IN THE NOTES.

ab = ex parte, 48
abhorrere a, 123
abiurare, 64
absque argumento, 116
abundare, 59
accipere, 113
―― pecuniam ob, 108
acclamatio, 91
aculeus, 111
Acutilius, 58, 60, 63
adeo, 108
adesse contra, 51
adfectus, 61
adfinis, 60
adflicta res publica, 112
adiudicare, 119
adiungere, 84
adlegatio, 69
admurmuro, 76
adpellare, 64, 68
adrogatio, 113
adsentiens, 124
adsiduus, 68
adventitia pecunia, 118
advocatus, 91
Aedui, 117
Aelia et Fufia, 101, 102
aerarii...aerati, 91
Agamemnon, 112
ager publicus, 118
agere ad populum, 70, 72
―― cum aliquo, 51, 77
agilitas, 105
Agraria lex, 115, 118
agrarii, 118
agripetae, 119
alienari, 107, 112

aliquando, 114
aliquid sermonis, 73
aliter accidere, 55
altercatio, 95
alterius praesidia, 123
Amalthea, 75
amans patriam, 117
ambitio, 53
ambitiosa, 111
ambulatio, 111
amplecti, 79
amplissimi homines, 53
ancoris sublatis, 74
annus egregius, 112
antiquare, 79
Antonius, C. 46, 70, 71, 76, 104
aperte tecte, 84
apud, 63, 75, 100, 120
Aquilius, 47
arbitrium, 68
arcae confidere, 65
Archias, 104
Areopagitae, 92
Argiletum, 87
Aristarchus, 83
Arpinas homo, 97
Arpinatia praedia, 62, 105
Arretini, 118
Arrius, 109
articulorum dolor, 62
Asia, 88, 103
Asiani, 108
asperum, 120
atriolum, 67
Atticus homo, 122
auctor legis, 118
auctoritas, 89, 93, 107, 122

INDEX.

Auli filius, 47, 99, 113, 125
aures nactus, 111
auspicio bono, 102
Autronius, L. 80
Axius, 70, 72

Baiae, 96
barbatuli, 85
beati, 81, 119
bellus, 53
beneficium, 76
bona venire, 51
bonae partes, 77
boni viri, 79, 124
bonitas, 105

Caecilius, 51, 70, 72
Caesar, L. I. 48
Caesonius, 47
Caieta, 57, 59
Calenus, Q. Fufius, 82, 89
Calvus, 92
candidatorium munus, 50
cantilena, 120
Catilina, L. Sergius, 47, 54, 96
Cato, 85, 107, 115
Catulus, Q. Lut. 77, 93, 124
cavillator, 77
causa, 111
—— non verecunda, 108
causam sustinere, 53
censeri absens, 114, 115
centesimae, 70, 72
Ceramicus, 66
certus, 48
Chilius, 65, 72, 104
Cicero, fil. 111
——, Luc. Tull. 60
Cincia lex, 125
Cincius, L. 46, 63
Circus Flaminius, 82
clamores, 84
claudus, 102
Clodius, P. 55, 73, 113, 123
cognoscere, 52
comis, 79
comissatores, 99
comitia mea, 67
commentarium, 120
committere ut, 62
communicatio, 106
comperisse omnia, 86

competitor, 50
concidere, 86
concordiam disiungere, 112
concursare, 85
concursus, 89
conducere de, 107
conglutinata concordia, 107, 109
coniectura provideri, 45
coniungi, 109
consentaneum, 124
conservare, 59
considere, 90
Considius, 70, 72
consilium, 82
consistere, 95
constantiam praestare, 120
consulere tempori, 53
contendere, 61
contra gratiam, 113
controversia, 63
conturbatus, 74
convenire ad, 92
conventus, 122
convicium, 85
copiosus, 107
Cornelius, 70
Cornificius, Q. 46, 78
Cornutus, C. 87
Cossinius, L. 122
Crassus, M. Lic. 59, 92
crebrior, 116
curator, 49
Curio, C. 86, 97
——, C. Scrib. 85, 97, 103
Curius, 49
custos, 73

de in comp. 65
debere se alicui, 46
decidere, 63
defensor, 77
degustare, 95
deliciae, 107
demitigari, 79
dependere, 65
designati, 70
despondere, 57, 67, 95
devorare spe, 98
dicacitas, 77
dicis causa, 113, 114
diem dare, 68
dignitas, 76

INDEX

discedere a, 106
discessit, 62
discessus, 93
disputare amanter, 123
dissensio ac discidium, 107
dissolutum, 120
dissuasor, 85
distineor, 81
divinitus, 95
divisores, 100, 113
dodrans, 87
dolo malo, 51
dolorem inurere, 94
Domitius, L. 52, 100
domum reduci, 92
domus, 98
Doterio, 100
dubiae res, 119
dum, with past tense, 90

ecquid tantum causae, 105
egestas, 89
elabi e manibus, 94
elaborare, 61
elegantiae, 64
en tellus! 110
Epicurean School, 56
epigrammata, 103
Epirotica, 62
esse ad scribendum, 122
exaedificata, 62
exagitatus, 112
excogitare, 89
excurrere, 50
exedrae, 64
exerceri, 70
exercitus noster, 118
exhaurire, 111, 119
existimatio, 48
—— summa, 53
—— populi, 59
expiari, 107
explicare, 108
exponere, 57
exprimere aliquid, 120
exsilium, 96

fabula Caeciliana, 104
—— Clodiana, 111
—— mimus, 103
facies...facetiae, 77
facultates, 81, 106

falsum, 96
Favonius, 86
fautores, 95
fieri pro populo, 78
Figulus, C. M. 54
filiolus, 54
firmamenta, 112
firmus, 48
fistula pastoricia, 99
Fonteius, 113
forensis, 60
Flavius, 118
flocci facteon, 103
fortuito gerere, 124
frater=patruelis, 60
fraudari, 51
frequentari, 118
frigere, 81
frontem ferire, 46
fructus, 60, 111
Frugi, C. Piso, 57
fucosae amicitiae, 111
fucus, 45

Galba, P. S. 45
Gallia, 50, 125
Gallicum bellum, 73
germanus, 117
gratiam inire, 83
gratus, 64, 81
grex Catilinae, 85
gymnasium, 54

hendiadys: instances, 60, 74
Herennius, 101, 113
Hermathena, 53
Hermeraclae, 66
Hilarus, 72
hirudo contionalis, 99
historiae, 122
hoc, 72
honorum studium, 106
Hortensius, 85, 89
humanitas, 60, 75
humaniter ferre, 54

iam, 74, 125
—— nunc, 64
—— vero, 93
Idaeus pastor, 112
idem, 69, 85
idoneus, 104

INDEX.

immittere, 96
immutari, 68, 120
impetrare nihil, 107
implicari amicitiis, 120
imprudens, 120
in buccam venire, 74
in officio manere, 56
inanis, 81
includere, 80
incommoditas, 106
incumbere ad, 118
induci, 108, 125
infirmus, 90
informare, 50
ingemere, 46
iniquitates, 70
inquiri apud, 100
insidere, 105, 111
insigne, 59
instaurare, 78
insusurrare, 120
intercedere, 90, 93
intercessio, 58
intermortui, 85
interpres, 73
is = talis, 59, 109
istim, 84
ita...ut, 46, 120
iucundus, 64, 81
iudicium constupratum, 112
iudicum inopia, 89
iurare morbum, 47
Iuventatis sacra, 112
iuventus delicata, 119

lacessitus, 75
laedere, 86
lanista, 90
Latinae, 56
laudatio, 119
lector, 74
legati 50, 117
legationes, 86, 115
lentius, nihil, 70, 113
Lentulus, 65
——, Cn. Corn. 117
levitas, 124
liber, 80
liberare agrum, 118
libertinus, 73
locatio, 107
loci esse, 63

Lucceius, L. 57, 64, 68
Lucullus, L. L. 51, 86, 104, 112
——, M. 104, 112
ludus talarius, 90
—— gladiatorius, 93
Lurco, M. Auf. 101
Lyceum, 64
Lycurgei, 79

Macer, C. Lic. 58
maculosus, 90
magister, 52
Magnus noster, 99, 125
mancipio, 51
mandare, 67
Manlius, T. 104
manus illa, 51
Marianae, 97
maturitas, 52
matutinum tempus, 111
maxima, 82
mederi, 120
medicinam refugere, 111
Megarica signa, 65
mellitus, 111
mendose fuisse, 80
mentionem facere, 96, 98
meridie non lucere, 47
Messala, M. Val. 87
Metellus, Q. 80, 92, 125
minus commode fieri, 103
mire quam, 70
missus est sanguis, 98
moderatissimus, 123
modeste, 109
mollis, 105
morosus, 77
Mucia, 73
munusculum, 64

Nanneiani, 93
nefas, 78
negare, 46
negociator, 116
negocium, 72, 81
nequam, 72, 119
nescire quid emerit, 119
nihil absoluti, 104
—— agere cum, 77
—— esse, 119
nobiles, 50
Nonae Decemb. 119

INDEX.

nostri equites, 107
nota et testificata, 106
nudus, 90
numarii iudices, 95
numos dividere, 113
numum movere, 70
nuncium remittere, 78

obducere, 49
obfirmatus, 69
obire comitia, 58
obiurgare senatum, 107
observare, 52
obtinere religionem, 107
offendere, 68
omittere provinciam, 107
operae, 79
operam dare, 78
operto, in, 97
oratio perpetua, 95
ornare, 107
ornatissime, 83
os praebere, 115

pacificator Allobrogum, 76
Paetus, L. Pap. 125
Palicanus, M. Loll. 48, 11
Panhormi, 120
Paris, 112
patronus, 92, 97
pecuniam cogere, 73
pedarii, 121, 125
Peducaeus, 58, 61
pellectio, 75
Pentelicus, 64
percrebrescit, 46
perdere omnia, 93
perhibere, 53
perhonorificus, 77
permittere, with dat. 67
permolestus, 111
perstringere, 84
perversus, 86
petitio, 45
petiturire, 88
Philadelphus, 70
Philippus, 100
piscinae, 113
piscinarii, 115, 119, 124
Piso, C. C. 50, 76, 86, 95
——, M. 77, 87, 89
Plancius, Cn. 73

Plautus, 94
Plotia lex, 115
plumbeo gladio, 90
Pompeia, 78
Pompeianum, 123
Pompeius, 70, 73, 79
Pomponia, 60
pontes, 85
Pontius, L. 52
populare, 118, 120, 123
portorium circumsectionis, 76
possessiones, 118
postulatio, 91
potestas, 69
praepropera, 46
praestare manum, 51
prensare, 45
primas deferre, 106
princeps, 107
pro populo fieri, 74
—— testimonio, 89
—— vectura solvere, 56
procurator, 58, 63
producere, 82
proeliari, 88
profici, with dat. 46
prolixa, 50
promulgare, 113, 114
pronunciare, 102
provincia, 117
proxime, with acc. 83
Pseudo-Cato, 87
publicani, 113
publicare, 118
pulchellus puer, 96
purgare se, 121
putealia, 67
putidum, 81

quaestus, 73
quicum...quocum, 110
quin, 107
—— imo, 77
Quintus frater, 58
quisquiliae, 94
quod infectum est, 78

Rabirius, C. 62
raptim currere, 125
ratio, 106, 107
ratiocinator, 73
rationibus conducere, 48

INDEX.

recidere in annum, 48
recolligi, 61
referre acceptum, 83
refrigescere, 50
regnum iudiciale, 47
reiecti, 58, 114
reiectio iudicum, 90
reiicere rationem, 118
relevare, 75
religio, 79, 107
relinquere, 104
requiescere, 111
reservare, 67
respicere, 94
respondere, 92
restituere, 66
retardari, 125
retinere in possessione, 118
revisere, 114
Rex, Q. Marc. 98
rhetorum, 75
Rhinton, 124
rogationem ferre, 79, 85
—— promulgare, 82

sal, 75
salus, 86
Sallustius, 57, 68
satis dare, 63
—— facere, 52, 118
Satrius, 51, 52
Saufeius, L. 56
Scipio, P. 52
scito, 109
scrupulus, 111
secundus, 107
secus dicitur, 121
Selicius, 70
sentina urbis, 119
Sequani, 117
sermo, 60
Servilius, P. fil. 122
servula, 74
Siculus ille, 120
Sicyon, 76, 121, 124
sigillata, 67
significatio parva, 108
Silanus, D. I. 48
simul = simul ac, 101
solitudo, 111, 118
sonitus, 84
sors mea, 117

sortiri, 117
splendor forensis, 111
Spongia, 94
sponsor, 64, 68
status dignitatis, 123
sub lustrum, 116
subesse, 66
subodiosum, 61
subtilius, 80
subvenitur rei, 107
succedi, 70
summa res publica, 95
summissum, 123
Sura, P. Lentulus, 95
suspiritus, 112

tabellae, 86
tabellarius, 70, 111
tabulae, 92
Tadius, 62
tamen, 90
tanti putare, 69
tectorium, 67
temeritas, 107
teneo, 61
tense, epistolary, 46, 104, 118
Terentia, 70, 71
terrae filius, 79
testimonium, 119
Thalna, 94
Thermus, Min. 48, 54
togula picta, 115
traducere, 113
tranquillitas temporum, 123
Tres Tabernae, 74
triumphare, 91, 125
trudere, 99
Tulliola, 57
tutela legitima, 62
typus, 67

unus, 45, 53
urbanae res, 118
urbanus = civilian, 50
usus = usu capio, 62
uti ad invidiam, 89
—— senatu, 107
uti rogas, 85

vacationes, 117
vafer, 120
valde vindicare, 104

INDEX.

Valerius, P. 73
varietas voluntatis, 105
vectigalia nova, 118
venditare, 88
venustas, 95
verecundia, 106
verumtamen = δ' οὖν, 66
vexare, 113
via Flaminia, 49
via munitur, 108
vici et prata, 59
victimis caesis, 75

vilitas, 85
vindemiolae, 67
vituperor, 121
Volaterrani, 118
voluntas ac iudicium, 107
—— institutae vitae, 106
—— perspecta, 107
—— secunda, 118
voluntates, 50

Xenocrates, 92
xysti, 64

www.ingramcontent.com/pod-product-compliance
Lightning Source LLC
Chambersburg PA
CBHW030332170426
43202CB00010B/1100